SUSHI SLIM

PHOTOGRAPHY
BY
LISA LINDER

BY
MAKIKO SANO

Aberdeenshire

Contents

寿司スリム法

How to Sushi Slim

Virtuous indulgence

Indulge and slim

Japanese food is healthy, delicious, good for you and helps you lose weight. For women in Japan, how, what and when they eat is seated in tradition, in the treasured ingredients of rice, miso, wasabi, fish, tea and seaweed that are the traditional harvests of our island nation. All of these have incredible slimming and beauty-boosting benefits.

The sushi, soup, salad and bento box recipes in this book are not only the height of food fashion, but also the perfect fast food for busy people on the run... and you will learn how simple they are to make.

And although people in the West might view the phrase 'healthy diet' with trepidation, bringing as it does connotations of abstinence and avoidance, our style of healthy eating is all about what I call Virtuous Indulgence. Japanese food is full of all the sensuous experiences you would normally feel deprived of on a western 'diet'. We eat first with our eyes: the food looks beautiful. Next up come touch, feel and texture, and finally the exquisite taste.

The Japanese culture of slimness

In Japan, we are taught from a really young age what is good for our bodies. It's part of our culture to eat healthy foods which help maintain a trim figure and improve our looks.

Unlike the Western sweep-it-under-the-carpet approach to weight gain, Japanese women openly scrutinise each other's figures and won't hesitate to mention if someone has added a few pounds. In fact it has even been legislated for, with the maximum waist size for a woman over 40 years old set at 90 centimetres. Some of Tokyo's restaurants have scales at each table; others serve 500-calorie lunches.

We may not have calorie-counting restaurants in the West (yet!), but this book will do the work for you. Each of the delicious dishes has been calorie counted, and our dietitian-devised diet plan will show how, by introducing just one Japanese meal a day into your diet, you can lose a healthy amount of weight each week, or just maintain your ideal weight. So, if you want to indulge your way to a healthier, trimmer, more glowing you, try Sushi Slim.

Japanese food:
The facts and your figure

Many Japanese people are taught to eat until they are 80 per cent full, and this might be one reason for their trim figures. In the latest world obesity rankings, Japan scored the second lowest percentage, with a mere 3.9 per cent, compared to America's troubling 33.8 per cent.

The average daily calorie intake in Japan is 2,754 kcal, compared to the USA's 3,825 kcal.

The Omega-3 content of the high prevalence of fish in the diet, along with a relatively small amount of meat eaten in Japan, is thought responsible for low levels of cardiovascular problems in the country.

They say variety is the spice of life. The typical Japanese person will have about 100 varieties of food per week, compared with just 30 in the average British diet, or 45 in the Mediterranean diet.

Results from a study at the end of 2011 suggested that a traditional Japanese diet may help to manage Type 2 diabetes mellitus.

For many years researchers have been aware of the extreme health and longevity benefits of a Japanese diet, especially the now legendary Okinawa way of eating, where inhabitants of the Japanese island regularly live to 100 (and an Okinawan was found to be 6.5 times less likely to die from breast cancer).

When you understand all that this cuisine offers, the only question about embracing a whole new style of eating is: why didn't I do it before?

Seven reasons why the Japanese diet will help you lose weight

1

Portion control

Because of the way in which it is presented, with three or four dishes, Japanese meals give the impression of being bigger than they are. At least one of the dishes will be a low-calorie, filling soup. In Western cuisine, the style is to use one big dinner plate groaning with quite a mountain of food. A typical set of sushi contains about 300 calories. An average Western plate of food can be 500 calories *more* than this.

2

Chopsticks

Slowing the rate at which you eat allows your brain to notice when you feel full. The Western eat-on-the-run way of dining means we have often overeaten before we even know it. Japanese people find it easier to notice when we are full because we use chopsticks, which are a more time-consuming way to eat. Set aside at least 20 minutes to eat each meal, as it takes your stomach about that time to register fullness.

3

Swerve dairy and meat

Japanese people do eat some meat, but not much of it compared to the Western diet. Also, dairy wasn't eaten in a traditional Japanese diet, and still isn't a big part of it. These two food stuffs are high in fat and responsible for much of the Western daily calorie intake.

4
Big breakfasts and early, light suppers

We often eat a selection of dishes in the morning: miso soup; rice; omelette; and grilled salmon (see page 76 if you'd like to try a Japanese breakfast). Japanese people also tend not to snack after 4pm, and eat an early supper that focuses on fish and vegetables. We also don't tend to eat desserts at home.

5
Green tea

Japanese people drink green tea throughout the day and it's readily available from street vending machines, which preheat it in cans. It contains virtually no calories. In contrast, the western equivalent — the ubiquitous coffee shop — is a diet baddie. Even if you order a skinny latte, you will take in around 100 calories, and that can increase to a staggering 500 calories for a mocha with cream.

6
Good things in small packages

Instead of tearing open a long roll of biscuits and ploughing through them, Japanese people tend to pick up snack-sized dainties. Small packaging minimises the temptation to overdo it. So, if you're wavering and feeling like you might blow your diet, pick up a mini pack of sesame snaps, or satisfyingly salty rice crackers. It's a simple idea, but a great damage limitation exercise.

7
Acid test

Sushi translates as 'vinegared rice'. Vinegar and other acetic acid-based pickles, ubiquitous in Japanese food, have a distinct effect on how we digest fat when eaten as part of a meal. Japanese researchers recently found that acetic acid may aid in fat burning. Another study found that vinegar taken after a high-GI food, such as white bread, not only reduced peaks in blood glucose, but also increased the feeling of fullness. When vinegar was introduced into a test diet, 10 per cent less body fat was produced.

Diamond ingredients

'Our foods are full of goodies. We say eating them makes us sparkle like diamonds... forever.'

The Japanese diet not only helps you to lose pounds and maintain a healthy weight, it's anti-ageing, bursting with complexion-boosting goodies and adds gloss and condition to your hair and nails.

Part of what makes Japanese food so different is the myriad of 'diamond' foods we use, that do so much more than taste great.

GINGER FOR ALL-ROUND HEALTH
This rhizome contains silicone to promote smooth and even skin tone, glossy hair and healthy teeth and nails. It is also considered to act as a mild aphrodisiac.

NORI FOR MERMAID LOCKS
This is the seaweed used to make sushi. It is believed to stimulate hair growth as it contains naturally high quantities of biotin, a compound often sold as a supplement in health food stores to strengthen hair.

SESAME SEEDS FOR A YOUTHFUL BODY
These are small but nutritionally mighty. They have a cholesterol-lowering effect. Sesamin, a compound found in the seeds, has also been found to protect the liver from oxidative damage. The seeds are high in copper, which strengthens blood vessels to promote healthy skin and hair. Crush them in a mortar and pestle to release the maximum health-giving qualities.

VINEGAR
Japanese rice vinegar is used to flavour sushi rice. Several studies have found it can suppress body fat accumulation (see point 7, left).

YUZU FOR YOUNGER SKIN
This fragrant citrus contains antioxidants, bioflavanoids and a high level of vitamin C (three times that of lemon). It's worth seeking out from Japanese stores, and use it in any of the recipes in the book that call for lemon or lime. Yuzu zest also contains nomilin, a compound which has relaxing properties. Japanese women rely on it to rejuvenate maturing skin. I love to use the juice in salad dressings, or the zest shaved into a dipping sauce, or into the bath!

Diet-boosting drinks

As crucial as the food to the Japanese diet are the drinks. From skin-revitalising soups to low-calorie tipples, what's in your glass or tea cup could have more impact on your Sushi Slim plan than you think.

Green tea

Green tea — the most popular tea in my restaurant — wins hands down in the calorie stakes against the Western fascination with dairy-laden hot drinks. It is virtually calorie-free. In fact, you could actually burn about 80 calories for every five cups of green tea you drink, due to the 'thermic effect' on the body of processing the drink.

We drink hot green tea with every meal, and even buy it ready-made in bottles. It also makes a refreshing drink served cold, over ice, in the warmer months.

Green tea is laden with antioxidants that help lower cholesterol

Green tea has antibacterial properties which sweeten the breath

Oolong tea

Japanese oolong tea is almost like our cup of coffee. More intensely flavoured than green tea, I tend to have one very strong cup in the morning to provide that same boost that a shot of coffee would.

Barley tea

Strict dieters such as my sister would choose Japanese barley tea for its reputed detox properties, drinking it as we would drink water in the west.

Shochu and sake

Women in Japan opt for these over a cold beer, as they don't have any wheat content. The drinks have reputations for minimising hangovers, and shochu has a mere 35 calories per 50ml shot. Sake, also low in calories, contains more than 20 kinds of amino acids. Amongst their benefits is slow ageing of the skin.

Japanese wonder soups

FROM TOP: Chicken Collagen Soup in cube form; Hearty Root Vegetable miso soup

Collagen soup

You may have noticed little sachets of liquid collagen being sold at beauty counters. But this is old news in Japan. A girlfriend of mine first made me Collagen Soup in my teens and I've been hooked ever since. Even the morning after drinking it, my skin looks firmer and plumper. And it's not my imagination: The Japanese Journal of Complementary and Alternative Medicine found that drinks containing 10g of collagen produced a 50 per cent observable effectiveness against wrinkles and skin moisture content within one week. The soup I prefer is made with fish, either salmon or grouper, and it isn't something you will find at Japanese restaurants in the West. You can find recipes on pages 78–81. I eat it twice a week. I often make a large batch and freeze it in cubes to use later.

Miso soup

In Japan we would quite happily have miso at every meal. I carry sachets of it in my handbag to have at my desk. There are many different ways to make the soup, so it never gets boring (see pages 72–75). Miso has high levels of umami — the savoury taste — and so is hugely appealing and very satisfying.

Miso contains only 30 calories per 240ml serving

The amino acids in miso help rid the body of harmful toxins

Miso has high levels of antioxidants, the goodies that clean up the 'free radical' cells responsible for ageing

Miso is rich in zinc and manganese, which help give glossy hair and healthy nails

Sushi Slim meal plan

Miki Symons MSc, Japanese-trained dietitian

I have devised three diet plans. Each replaces just one meal a day in a normal Western diet with a delicious Japanese meal from Sushi Slim (though you can swap in two meals a day if you want... and it's easy to get hooked!).

On the Sushi Slim plan, you should aim to lose no more than two pounds each week. A slow, steady weight loss, along with taking regular exercise, is the best way to long-term success. Crash diets never work. It is also important to eat a morning and an afternoon snack, to keep you feeling full and avoiding temptation.

I advise that everyone considering a weight-loss diet should check with their GP first, just to rule out any problems. And always remember to drink lots of water throughout the day.

How many calories you should eat each day depends on how tall you are and whether you are aiming to lose weight, or simply maintain your figure. You can work out your calorie target using this sum, which I find helpful:

CALCULATE YOUR DAILY CALORIE TARGET

TO LOSE WEIGHT

HEIGHT × **HEIGHT** × **20*** × **25** =
DAILY CALORIE TARGET

*target weight loss BMI

A person who is 161cm tall will need:
1.61 x 1.61 x 20 x 25 = 1,296 kcal every day
But a taller 173cm person will need more calories:
1.73 x 1.73 x 20 x 25 = 1,496 kcal every day

TO MAINTAIN WEIGHT

HEIGHT × **HEIGHT** × **22**** × **25** =
DAILY CALORIE TARGET

**target weight maintenance BMI

In our two examples, the shorter and taller people will need:
1.61 x 1.61 x 22 x 25 = 1,426 kcal every day
1.73 x 1.73 x 22 x 25 = 1,646 kcal every day

You should remember that, in order to lose weight, you need to work out your daily calorie intake using the first sum, to give a lower total. As you slim, and move to maintaining weight, you can increase your calorie intake according the second sum.

I have given plans for 1,300 calories, 1,500 calories and 1,700 calories. I have also given calorie counts for every meal, in case you need to fine-tune your daily calorie target. I have rounded off all calorie counts to the nearest five calories, for ease.

CHOOSE FROM:

1,300 kcal/day

300 kcal breakfast

CEREAL AND TOAST
Cup of coffee or tea with semi-skimmed milk **+15 kcal**
30g bowl of cereal or porridge with semi-skimmed milk **+150 kcal**
Thin slice of wholemeal toast **+60 kcal**
½ tbsp jam **+25 kcal**
1 tsp butter **+35 kcal**

FRUIT AND YOGURT
Cup of coffee or tea with semi-skimmed milk **+15 kcal**
100g pot fat-free yogurt **+70 kcal**
100g mango **+65 kcal**
100g pineapple **+55 kcal**
100g raspberries **+40 kcal**
150g melon **+50 kcal**

EGG AND BACON
Cup of coffee or tea with semi-skimmed milk **+15 kcal**
Thin slice of wholemeal toast **+60 kcal**
1 tsp butter **+35 kcal**
2 small poached eggs **+120 kcal**
2 rashers of grilled back bacon **+70 kcal**

100 kcal snack

Green tea **+0 kcal**
Small banana **+75 kcal**
Handful of strawberries, about 5 **+25 kcal**
OR
Green tea **+0 kcal**
Medium handful of almonds, about 10 **+70 kcal**
1 medium satsuma **+30 kcal**

500 kcal lunch

Sushi Slim options

BENTO BOX LUNCHES
Unlimited green tea **+0 kcal**
Bento Box (choose from 10 different boxes) all **+460–510 kcal**

SUSHI LUNCH — *2 choices*
Unlimited green tea **+0 kcal**
Monk Rolls, 4 pieces **+510 kcal**

Unlimited green tea **+0 kcal**
Basic Miso Soup **+30 kcal**
Tempura King Prawn and Avocado California rolls, 6 pieces **+460 kcal**

COLLAGEN SOUP LUNCH
Unlimited green tea **+0 kcal**
1 bowl Chicken Collagen Soup, with shredded chicken **+300 kcal**
1 portion Lightly Grilled Tuna with Rocket **+165 kcal**
handful of strawberries (about 10) **+50 kcal**

Western options

SANDWICH AND SOUP
Small cheese salad sandwich **+300 kcal**
Vegetable and bean soup **+190 kcal**

RAMEN NOODLES
Grilled salmon ramen soup noodles **+465 kcal**

TOASTIE, SALAD AND FRUIT
1 slice cheese on toast with 40g cheddar, plus large mixed salad with 2 tsp dressing **+300 kcal**
large apple **+100 kcal**
medium banana **+100 kcal**

SALAD AND YOGURT POT
Tuna Niçoise salad with dressing **+300 kcal**
120g yogurt and granola pot **+185 kcal**

300 kcal dinner

Sushi Slim options

SUSHI — *6 choices*
Tuna and Cucumber California rolls, 6 pieces **+335 kcal**
Red and Yellow Pepper, Onion and Mushroom gunkan, 6 pieces **+290 kcal**
Avocado and Chilli hosomaki rolls, 6 pieces **+300 kcal**
Crab Stick and Lettuce hosomaki rolls, 6 pieces **+255 kcal**
Salmon nigiri, 6 pieces **+330 kcal**
Avocado nigiri, 6 pieces **+320 kcal**

SOUP AND SALAD — *2 choices*
Tofu and Seaweed Miso Soup **+45 kcal**
1 portion Tuna and Avocado Tartare **+230 kcal**

Aubergine miso soup **+35 kcal**
2 portions of Steamed Vegetables with Creamy Tofu Dressing **+220 kcal**

Western options

OMELETTE AND SALAD
Omelette made with 2 eggs, 1 tsp oil and 1 tbsp chopped ham **+225 kcal**
Mixed salad (unlimited amount) with 2 tsp dressing **+75 kcal**

PASTA AND SAUCE
50g (raw weight) pasta **+175 kcal**
100g Bolognese sauce (made with lean minced meat) **+140 kcal**
OR
75g (raw weight) pasta **+260 kcal**
125g tomato-based sauce **+50 kcal**
Plus unlimited steamed vegetables **+negligible kcal**

GRILLED CHICKEN AND VEG
1 large chicken breast **+130 kcal**
1 small aubergine **+20 kcal** plus 1 red pepper **+50 kcal** roasted with 1 tbsp olive oil **+120 kcal**

CURRY AND RICE
180g cooked brown rice **+200 kcal**
100g vegetable curry **+100 kcal**
Plus unlimited steamed vegetables **+negligible kcal**

CHOOSE FROM:

1,500 kcal/day

400 kcal breakfast

EGGS
Cup of coffee or tea with semi-skimmed milk **+15kcal**
Scrambled eggs made with 3 large eggs **+225 kcal** and 5g butter **+35 kcal**
1 medium slice wholemeal toast **+85 kcal**
with 1 tsp butter **+35 kcal**

FRUIT, NUTS, SEEDS AND YOGURT
Cup of coffee or tea with semi-skimmed milk **+15kcal**
200g 2% Greek yogurt **+150kcal**
190g fresh fruit salad **+115kcal**
25g mixed nuts and seeds **+150kcal**

TOAST AND APPLE
Cup of coffee or tea with semi-skimmed milk **+15kcal**
2 medium slices wholemeal toast **+170kcal**
2 tsp butter **+70kcal**
1 tbsp jam **+50kcal**
1 small apple **+90kcal**

100 kcal snack

Unlimited green tea **+0 kcal**
Small banana **+75kcal**
Medium satsuma **+30kcal**
OR
Unlimited green tea **+0 kcal**
Tofu and Seaweed miso soup **+45kcal**
Large handful of strawberries, about 10 **+50kcal**

500 kcal lunch

Sushi Slim options

BENTO BOX LUNCHES
Unlimited green tea **+0 kcal**
Bento Box (choose from 10 different boxes) **all +460 – 510 kcal**

SUSHI LUNCH — *2 choices*
Unlimited green tea **+0 kcal**
Avocado and Chilli hosomaki rolls, 6 pieces **+300 kcal**
Oil-free Edamame, about 30 pods **+50 kcal**
200g tropical fruit salad **+145 kcal**

Unlimited green tea **+0 kcal**
Tempura King Prawn and Avocado California roll, 6 pieces **+460 kcal**
Basic Miso Soup **+30 kcal**

COLLAGEN SOUP LUNCH
Unlimited green tea **+0 kcal**
Chicken Collagen Soup, with shredded chicken **+300 kcal**
1 portion Aubergine and Shallot Salad **+156 kcal**
125g raspberries **+60 kcal**

Western options

SANDWICH AND SOUP
Hummus and vegetable sandwich **+400 kcal**
Tomato and vegetable soup, without dairy **+100 kcal**

PIZZA AND SALAD
½ medium (20cm) marguerita pizza **+410 kcal**
Salad with 2 tsp dressing **+75 kcal**

WRAP AND FRUIT
Chargrilled chicken wrap **+410 kcal**
1 small apple **+90 kcal**

SALAD AND MUFFIN
Tuna salad with reduced-calorie dressing **+200 kcal**
Low-fat blueberry muffin **+300 kcal**

400 kcal dinner

Sushi Slim options

SUSHI — *3 choices*
3 Hint of Lime hand rolls **+410 kcal**
2 Suzu Yellowtail hand rolls **+405 kcal**
8 pieces mixed fish nigiri **about +400 kcal**

SOUP AND SALAD — *2 choices*
1 portion Lightly Grilled Tuna with Rocket **+165kcal**
1 portion Facelift-in-a-bowl **+210kcal**

Spicy Pork miso soup **+100kcal**
1 portion Steamed Sesame Chicken Salad **+245kcal**

Western options

GRILLED FISH AND ROASTED VEGETABLES
120g salmon fillet, grilled **+250kcal**
200g mixed roast vegetables **+130kcal**

GNOCCHI WITH TOMATO AND OLIVE SAUCE
150g plain gnocchi **+230kcal**
100g tomato and olive pasta sauce **+150kcal**

COUSCOUS AND VEGETABLE TAGINE
150g cooked couscous **+175kcal**
400g vegetable tagine **+220kcal**

BAKED POTATO AND CHEESE
1 medium baked potato **+160kcal**
60g grated Cheddar cheese **+250kcal**

1,700 kcal/day

500 kcal breakfast

LATTE AND BACON ROLL
Large whole milk latte (no syrup, no cream) **+135kcal**
Brown bread roll **+145kcal**
3 rashers of grilled back bacon **+105kcal**
2 tsp butter **+70kcal**

CEREAL AND TOAST
Cup of coffee or tea with semi-skimmed milk **+15kcal**
30g bowl of cereal or porridge with semi-skimmed milk **+150kcal**
2 medium slices wholemeal toast **+170kcal**
2 tsp butter **+70kcal**
1 tbsp jam **+50kcal**

HAM, CHEESE AND RYE BREAD
Cup of coffee or tea with semi-skimmed milk **+15kcal**
3 slices rye bread **+165kcal**
2 slices emmental cheese **+240kcal**
75g smoked or unsmoked ham **+80kcal**

100 kcal snack

Unlimited green tea **+0 kcal**
Large handful of almonds, about 15 **+100kcal**
OR
Unlimited green tea **+0 kcal**
Basic Miso Soup **+30 kcal**
Large handful of cherries, about 10 **+70kcal**

500 kcal lunch

Sushi Slim options

BENTO BOX LUNCHES
Unlimited green tea **+0 kcal**
Bento Box (choose from 10 different boxes) **all +460–510 kcal**

HOSOMAKI FEAST
Crab Stick and Lettuce, 6 pieces **+255 kcal**
Canned Tuna and Spring Onion, 6 pieces **+245 kcal**

CHILLI HEAD
Spicy Salmon California rolls, 6 pieces **+450 kcal**
Basic Miso Soup **+30 kcal**

OMEGA-3 HIT
2 x Omega-3 Hit hand rolls **+445 kcal**
Basic Miso Soup **+30 kcal**

Western options

BIG TOASTIE
Sandwich chain large cheese and onion toastie **+500 kcal**

CHEESE SALAD PACK
Feta, lentil and rice salad **+520 kcal**

RAMEN NOODLES
Large bowl chicken ramen **+520 kcal**

LETTUCE WRAP 'BURGER'
Beef burger wrapped in lettuce, without bread **+475 kcal**

500 kcal dinner

Sushi Slim options

FACELIFT SOUP AND SUSHI
1 bowl Facelift-in-a-bowl **+210 kcal**
Okra and Sesame California rolls, 6 pieces **295 kcal**

SALAD
Fill-you-up Soba Noodle Salad **+500 kcal**

JAPANESE BREAKFAST-FOR-DINNER
Fish, rice, omelette, miso soup, pickles **+560 kcal**

TERIYAKI AND RICE
1 portion Chicken Teriyaki **+195 kcal**
200g cooked brown rice **+220 kcal**
Plus unlimited steamed vegetables **+negligible kcal** with 2 tsp butter **+70kcal**

Western options

ROAST VEGETABLES WITH RICE AND FRUIT SALAD
350g roast vegetable salad **+220 kcal**
180g cooked brown rice **+200 kcal**
190g fresh fruit salad **+85 kcal**

CHICKEN CURRY
125g dry tandoori chicken **+240 kcal**
180g cooked brown rice **+200 kcal**
1 tbsp mango chutney **+60 kcal**

STIR-FRIED PRAWNS AND VEGETABLES
1 portion, made with splash of oil **+300 kcal**
175g cooked rice noodles **+190 kcal**

STEAK AND SALAD
175g sirloin steak **+240 kcal**
baked sweet potato **+175 kcal**
2 tsp French dressing **+75kcal**
Unlimited green salad **+negligible kcal**

FOOLPROOF SUSHI

きほん

How to make perfect sushi rice
How to cut vegetables
How to choose and cut fish
Secrets of a Japanese storecupboard

HOW TO MAKE PERFECT SUSHI RICE

600ml short-grain sushi rice (this is best measured by volume)
120ml sushi rice seasoning vinegar (Clearspring make a good version)

You will need a large, shallow bowl, or an oven tray or large serving plate.

HOW TO COOK RICE

Find a large pan with a tight-fitting lid. Wash the rice thoroughly, then leave it in a sieve to dry for at least 30 minutes.

Measure 660ml of water and pour it into your pan. Add the rice. Place over a medium heat, cover, and leave it for 10–13 minutes, until it comes to a boil (listen for the bubbles; do not remove the lid).

When the water has come to a boil, reduce the heat to its lowest for 30 seconds, then turn the heat off. Leave it for 15 minutes with the lid on.

Now it's ready.

HOW TO SEASON SUSHI RICE

Put the hot rice in your bowl, tray or other container, sprinkle on the rice seasoning vinegar fairly evenly and mix it in gently but really well with a broad wooden or plastic spoon or spatula.

Cool it down with a fan, turning the rice carefully, to let every grain of rice soak up all the vinegar.

Leave it for 10–15 minutes until the rice is cool to the touch, but not too cold.

You are now ready to make sushi, or to freeze the rice in handy portion sizes.

MAKING BROWN SUSHI RICE

You can make brown sushi rice with exactly the same quantities and method. The only difference is that brown sushi rice needs to be soaked.

Soak it in the measured amount of cooking water (see recipe, far left) for at least 4 hours before cooking. The easiest way to do this is to put it to soak in the morning, and cook it when you get home from work.

HOW TO CUT VEGETABLES

**All vegetables for sushi rolls are ultimately cut into slender sticks.
Think of cutting most vegetables for sushi rolls into 6cm strips. A cucumber needs to be
cut in half lengthways, then cut in half again, deseeded, then cut lengthways to form batons.
Vegetables for other sushi, and for salads, need to be treated differently, but do take time
in their preparation, as a neat, attractive appearance is very important in Japanese food.**

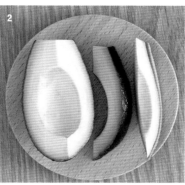

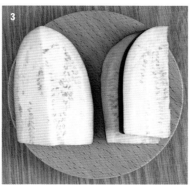

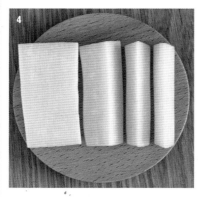

1 Cucumber cut for sushi rolls / **2** Avocado cut for sushi rolls / **3** Aubergine cut for nigiri (see page 46)
4 Mooli cut for salad (see page 83) / **5** Carrot cut for soup (see page 75)

HOW TO CHOOSE FISH

Most supermarkets now have fresh fish counters. Always pick up your fish from here rather than from the pre-packed shelves, as being wrapped in cling film can make the fish sweat. Whole fish can be easily filleted at the fish counter if you ask.

It's easy to spot fresh fish. The gills should be bright pink, not dark purple. The eyes should look clear and not grey or filmy.

Buying a whole salmon is not practical for home, so when choosing salmon fillet make sure it looks plump and firm. It's the same with tuna, which should be nice and red, not dark purple. When you cut it, the flesh should still look red, not silvery. If it smells too fishy or feels slimy, don't use it. Any fish used for sushi must be super-fresh; ask for 'sushi grade'.

I always rinse my fish in salty water and pat dry with strong kitchen paper before use. A lot of chefs don't bother, but I prefer to do this, as I feel it purifies and firms the flesh.

Try and buy fresh whole raw prawns, which you can quickly cook yourself (see page 40). However, if you are in a rush, you can buy pre-cooked prawns. Always remove the black digestive tract, a string that runs down the back of the prawn, and discard.

HOW TO CUT FISH FOR SUSHI

CUTTING TUNA FROM A BLOCK
1 Cut for sushi rolls / **2** Cut for sashimi / **3** Cut for nigiri (see overleaf for details)

HOW TO CUT FISH FOR SUSHI

TUNA

Start with a block of fresh tuna (ask the fishmonger for 'sushi-grade'). It should be red with no discolouration, firm, and should not smell too fishy.

For sushi rolls, cut 1cm sticks from the side of the block, against the grain of the fish as far as possible. Cut them into roughly 6cm lengths before use.

For nigiri, cut thin diagonal slices, 5mm thick, working across the grain of the fish and using a long, stroking action. Each of the slices will show the grain.

For sashimi, cut slices vertically to the board, each about 1cm thick, working across the grain of the fish. Make the slices as uniform as possible.

TO FILLET, SKIN AND CUT WHOLE FISH

 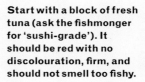   

Using 'sushi-grade' fish, stroke a slim, sharp and flexible blade along one side of the spine. With the knife flat, stroke the blade over the bones to release the fillet. Turn and repeat.

Lay a fillet skin-down. Insert a knife between skin and flesh at one end, grab the skin with your free hand, angle the blade to the work top, and push it to the end of the fillet.

For sashimi, cut slices vertically to the board, about 1cm thick. The slices should look pearly and display the attractive pattern of the grain.

For nigiri, cut thin diagonal slices, 5mm thick, working across the grain of the fish and using a long, stroking action. Each of the slices will show the grain.

SALMON

When choosing salmon fillets, go for 'sushi-grade' pieces that are bright, with no discolouration, and of a good, thick size for sushi. Cut in half lengthways.

The thinner part of the fillet is more suitable for cutting for sushi rolls. The more widely spaced grain of the thicker part is better for nigiri and sashimi.

Leave the thick part for cutting into 5mm slices on the diagonal for nigiri, and vertical 1cm slices for sashimi (both cut as for tuna, see left).

Cut the thinner part into 1cm sticks for sushi rolls. Be as even and uniform as possible. When you come to use them, cut them into roughly 6cm sections.

MACKEREL, OR ANY COOKED OR CURED FISH

Mackerel is tasty and very healthy, but must be spanking fresh. Peel off the parchment-like skin with your fingers, as it can harbour bacteria.

A piece of Marinated Mackerel (see page 59) will look different to raw fish, being opaque. It is flaky, so hard to cut; you'll need your sharpest knife.

For nigiri or sashimi, start at the tail end of the fillet and cut very thin slices on the diagonal, holding the fish with your free hand to prevent it flaking away.

Turn the slices as you cut them, and lay them out on the board. Despite it having been skinned, mackerel slices will retain an attractive pattern.

SECRETS OF A JAPANESE STORECUPBOARD

A one-stop trip to a Japanese store can stock your kitchen cupboard with authentic Japanese goodies. These have a long shelf life and can be relied upon to add amazing flavour in seconds.

1
NORI SEAWEED SHEETS
Essential for rolling sushi, these sheets of shredded, dried seaweed have a pleasing crispness and a neutral, slightly seaside flavour.

 2
WASABI PASTE
The ubiquitous, eye-watering sushi accompaniment, this paste is made from a root not dissimilar to Western horseradish. Make sure yours is not too bright green nor too cheap, as there are fakes on the market.

 3
WAKAME SEAWEED
Another edible seaweed, this is usually sold dried and shredded. It is great in salad (see page 89), or used as a topping for gunkan (see page 66).

 4
RICE SEASONING VINEGAR
A sweetened vinegar used mostly to season sushi rice. This is worth buying as it is more convenient than making your own seasoning mixture from scratch.

 5
SAKE
A dry rice wine, those you find in supermarkets (such as in the green bottle in the photo, left) are only good for cooking.

 6
DRIED SOBA (BUCKWHEAT) NOODLES
These cook in minutes so they are great storecupboard ingredients, and perfect if you need a quick meal. They also make a great salad (see page 87).

 7
JAPANESE SHORT-GRAIN RICE
Look for this in larger supermarkets. It is often labelled 'sushi rice' and stores for ages. Brown sushi rice is not as common as white, but is worth seeking out when you Sushi Slim, as it will keep you feeling full for longer.

 8
SESAME OIL
With a distinctive nutty taste, this oil is a wonderful accent for foods. Do not cook with it over a high heat, or its flavour will dissipate.

 9
DASHI or BONITO FLAKES
These fish flakes are everywhere in Japanese cuisine. They provide a savoury note to soups, omelettes, stocks and salad dressings.

 10
SUSHI ROLLING MATS
Essential for rolling hosomaki and California rolls (see pages 29–39), these are also light and easy to store.

 11
LIGHT SOY SAUCE
Made from fermented soy beans, this is one of the most essential tastes of Japanese foods, replacing salt in most recipes.

 12
MISO PASTE
An unique flavour and increasingly popular in the West. This paste, made from fermented soy beans, is hugely versatile: add to dishes, or use to make a quick soup.

EAT SUSHI – FEEL GREAT

*Wasabi is known for
its detox qualities, so you can feel purified
as you enjoy its hot, spicy flavour.*

Rolls

Quick and easy sushi

HOSOMAKI
Step-by-step: how to make hosomaki rolls

Salmon
Tuna and chive
Crab stick and lettuce
Canned tuna and spring onion
Avocado and chilli
Bacon and asparagus
Green bean and miso
Corned beef and sweetcorn

CALIFORNIA ROLLS
Step-by-step: how to make California rolls

Smoked salmon, wasabi cream cheese and lemon
Tempura prawn and avocado
Sesame prawn
Spicy salmon
Tuna and cucumber
Salmon and avocado
Tofu and pickles
Lettuce and pickled ginger
Okra and sesame

HIGH ROLLER

Wrap your sushi rolling mat in a layer of cling film
to keep it spotlessly clean and hygienic, changing
the cling film between different rolls.

HOW TO MAKE HOSOMAKI ROLLS

Cucumber roll

½ sheet of nori seaweed (halved horizontally)
130g prepared sushi rice (see page 20, about the size of 2 medium eggs)
2 cucumber batons

223 kcal per roll (6 pieces)

Place the seaweed near the bottom of a sushi rolling mat, rough side up and shiny side down. Place the rice in the middle of the seaweed.

Spread it out gently with your fingers to form an even covering all over the seaweed, leaving a 1cm strip empty at the top edge furthest from you.

Place the cucumber in a straight line, left to right, across the middle of the rice. You are now ready to roll.

Gently slide both thumbs under the mat and rest your middle fingers on the cucumber. Lift the edge of the mat and seaweed nearest to you over the cucumber.

Lift up the leading edge of the mat with your right hand, if you are right-handed. (Or simply reverse all the instructions.) Roll, with your left hand supporting the roll. Pull gently on the mat with your right hand.

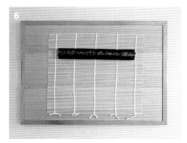

Gently squeeze the mat to form a tight roll. Remove the mat. With a very sharp knife, cut the roll in half. Put the halves together and cut into 6 pieces in total, wiping the blade between each cut.

A classic small roll, perfect for bite-sized snacks, or popping into a bento box.

HOSOMAKI ROLLS

For each hosomaki roll (each roll makes 6 pieces), you will need:

½ sheet of nori seaweed (halved horizontally)
130g prepared sushi rice (see page 20)

To make the hosomaki rolls, refer to the step-by-step guide (see page 31).

SALMON

2 salmon strips (see page 25)

281 kcal per roll (6 pieces)

TUNA AND CHIVE

2 tuna strips (see page 24)
5–6 chives, cut into 6cm lengths

256 kcal per roll (6 pieces)

CRAB STICK AND LETTUCE

2 crab sticks
1 tsp cream cheese
2 lettuce leaves

256 kcal per roll (6 pieces)

CANNED TUNA AND SPRING ONION

2 tbsp canned tuna in brine, drained
1 shredded spring onion

243 kcal per roll (6 pieces)

AVOCADO AND CHILLI

2 avocado slices
½ tsp chilli powder (ideally Japanese
chilli powder)

300 kcal per roll (6 pieces)

BACON AND ASPARAGUS

2 rashers of grilled back bacon
4 asparagus spears, blanched in salted water
for 3 minutes

310 kcal per roll (6 pieces)

GREEN BEAN AND MISO

30g green beans, blanched in salted water
for 3 minutes
1 tsp miso paste

240 kcal per roll (6 pieces)

CORNED BEEF AND SWEETCORN

2 tbsp canned corned beef
2 tsp sweetcorn kernels

260 kcal per roll (6 pieces)

HOW TO MAKE CALIFORNIA ROLLS

Salmon and avocado roll

½ sheet of nori seaweed (halved horizontally)
160g prepared sushi rice (see page 20, about the size of a medium avocado)
1 tsp black sesame seeds
2 salmon strips (see page 25)
2 avocado slices

408 kcal per roll (6 pieces)

Place the seaweed near the bottom of a sushi rolling mat, rough side up and shiny side down. Place the sushi rice in the middle of the seaweed.

Spread the rice out gently with your fingers to form an even covering all over the seaweed. Press on the sesame seeds, or other coverings, so they stick.

Carefully turn over the whole piece, rice and seaweed, so the seaweed is on top. Add the salmon and avocado slices, or other fillings, across the middle.

Gently slide both thumbs under the mat and rest your middle fingers on the filling. Lift the edge of the mat and seaweed nearest to you over the filling.

Lift up the leading edge of the mat with your right hand, if you are right-handed. (Or simply reverse all the instructions.) Roll, with your left hand supporting the roll. Pull gently on the mat with your right hand.

Gently squeeze the mat to form a tight roll. Remove the mat. With a very sharp knife, cut the roll in half. Put the halves together and cut into 6 pieces in total, wiping the blade between each cut.

This American version of sushi is bright and colourful. My recipes ditch the heavy use of mayo and cream cheese in commercial California rolls, but add more creaminess with avocado and a touch of cream cheese, if you like (though you'll increase the calories).

CALIFORNIA ROLLS

For each California roll (each roll makes 6 pieces), you will need:

½ sheet of nori seaweed
160g prepared sushi rice

To make the California rolls, refer to the step-by-step guide (see left).

SMOKED SALMON, WASABI CREAM CHEESE AND LEMON

For the covering
40g smoked salmon slices
6 very fine slices of unwaxed lemon

For the filling
1 tbsp wasabi cream cheese
(see page 58)
20g smoked salmon slices,
cut into slim lengths

422 kcal per roll (6 pieces)

TEMPURA PRAWN AND AVOCADO

For the covering
2 tsp tobiko (flying fish roe)
½ tsp black and white sesame seeds

For the filling
2 pieces King Prawn Tempura
(see page 40)
2 avocado slices
½ tsp shredded spring onion

460 kcal per roll (6 pieces)

SESAME PRAWN

For the covering
4 cooked, shelled and de-veined
prawns (see page 40)
½ tsp black and white sesame seeds

For the filling
2 cucumber batons
2 avocado slices

355 kcal per roll (6 pieces)

SPICY SALMON

For the covering
40g minced salmon
1 tsp chilli powder (ideally Japanese chilli powder)
1½ tsp mayonnaise

For the filling
2 avocado slices
2 cucumber batons

Simply mix the covering ingredients.

452 kcal per roll (6 pieces)

TUNA AND CUCUMBER

For the covering
½ tsp black and white sesame seeds

For the filling
2 tuna strips (see page 24)
2 cucumber batons

335 kcal per roll (6 pieces)

SALMON AND AVOCADO

For the covering
2 tbsp tobiko (flying fish roe)

For the filling
2 salmon strips (see page 25)
2 avocado slices

400 kcal per roll (6 pieces)

TOFU AND PICKLES

For the covering
3 shiso leaves (or rocket leaves)

For the filling
1 tbsp Japanese pickle
15g tofu, cut into strips

288 kcal per roll (6 pieces)

LETTUCE AND PICKLED GINGER

For the filling
10g lettuce leaves
1 tbsp pickled ginger

284 kcal per roll (6 pieces)

OKRA AND SESAME

For the covering
½ tsp black and white sesame seeds

For the filling
2–3 fingers of okra, blanched in salted
water for 2 minutes

295 kcal per roll (6 pieces)

Prawns for sushi

HOW TO COOK PRAWNS FOR NIGIRI

Start with shell-on king prawns. Insert a slim bamboo skewer into each, from underneath the tail, running up the belly to the head end. The idea is that the skewer keeps the prawn straight.

Bring a large pan of salted water to a boil and add the prawns on their skewers. Return to a boil and cook for 1 minute, or until completely pink, then drain and leave for 10 minutes.

Peel the prawns and discard the shell and head, but leave the tail in place. Score the flesh of each prawn up the belly, and open it out like a book.

Soak the prawns in sushi rice seasoning vinegar, turning to coat all sides. Like this, covered, they can be kept in the fridge for 2 to 3 days. Blot the prawns dry before use.

9 kcal per prawn

KING PRAWN TEMPURA

For the batter
100g self-raising flour
25g cornflour
½ tbsp baking powder
½ tsp salt

For the tempura
vegetable oil, to deep-fry
(about 1 litre)
12 raw king prawns, deveined,
tail left on

For the tempura sauce
50ml light soy sauce
50ml mirin
1 tsp bonito flakes

Sift all the ingredients for the batter into a bowl and pour in 150ml of cold water, whisking to combine. Heat the oil to 180°C (350°F) in a deep pan (you will need an oil thermometer to check the temperature).

Coat the prawns in the batter, then drop into the oil for 3 minutes. Do not crowd the pan; cook in batches if necessary. Remove with a slotted spoon and drain on kitchen paper.

Meanwhile, for the sauce, put all the ingredients in a pan, pour in 200ml of water and bring to the boil. Serve warm with the tempura.

Serves 2
354 kcal per serving, **708 kcal** in total

Although we use batter, the Japanese version is much lighter than a Western one. Tempura sauce just gives the dish that extra treat factor. Feel free to substitute the prawns with slices of sweet potato, carrot, aubergine or broccoli, for a vegetarian version.

Nigiri

The original sushi

NIGIRI
Step-by-step: how to make nigiri

Tuna
Salmon
Sea bream
Prawn
Grilled asparagus
Aubergine
Avocado
Okra and salted plum

SMOOTH CUSTOMER

*Rub oil into your palms and fingers when making
nigiri, so the sushi rice won't stick. Use a
neutral-tasting oil, and avoid olive or sesame oil.*

HOW TO MAKE NIGIRI

Prawn

trace of grapeseed oil or mayonnaise
12g prepared sushi rice (see page 20, about the size of a medium cherry)
1 cooked prawn (see page 40)

45 kcal per piece

Rub the grapeseed oil or mayonnaise
into your palms and fingers. Take the rice
in your right hand, if you are right-handed.
(Or simply reverse all the instructions.)
Hold the prawn (or other topping) in your
left hand, across the base of your fingers.

Place the rice on top of the fish. Put your
right index finger on top of the rice. Wrap
your left hand around your right index finger,
squeezing gently to make a nice shape. Turn
your nigiri so the fish is on top, still placed
over the base of the fingers.

Repeat the wrapping and squeezing steps
to form a neat, compact piece of nigiri.
Do not squash the rice together too hard;
all your movements should be gentle.

Now smooth the edges of the prawn or other
topping into an organic, graceful curve, with
no corners: the topping should drape
elegantly over the rice.

These are the favourite sushi in Japan, and were the first type. They are dainty and bite-sized. Each recipe below makes 1 piece, simply scale up to make as many as you want.

NIGIRI

For each piece of nigiri, you will need:

trace of grapeseed oil or mayonnaise
12g prepared sushi rice (see page 20, the size of a medium cherry)

To make the nigiri, refer to the step-by-step guide (see page 43).

TUNA

15g tuna, sliced for nigiri (see page 24), for each piece

42 kcal per piece

SALMON

15g salmon, sliced for nigiri (see page 25), for each piece

55 kcal per piece

SEA BREAM

15g sea bream, sliced for nigiri (see page 24),
for each piece

40 kcal per piece

PRAWN

1 cooked prawn (see page 40), for each piece

45 kcal per piece

GRILLED ASPARAGUS

2 asparagus spears, grilled for 3 minutes on each side, for each piece
1cm-thick strips of nori seaweed, for holding the asparagus in place

29 kcal per piece

AUBERGINE

10g Japanese aubergine slice, grilled for 3 minutes on each side, for each piece
sprinkling of finely grated root ginger
scattering of very finely chopped spring onion

Gently press the ginger and spring onion on to the rice, then add the aubergine slice.

28 kcal per piece

AVOCADO

15g thinly sliced avocado, for each piece

53 kcal per piece

OKRA AND SALTED PLUM

okra fingers, blanched in salted water for
2 minutes, then halved, ½ for each piece
tiny cubes of Japanese salted plum

33 kcal per piece

Social sushi

HAND ROLLS
Step-by-step: how to make hand rolls

Make a wish
Monk roll
Fig surprise
Hint of lime
New York dream
Suzu yellowtail
Prawn heaven
Omega-3 hit

GUNKAN
Step-by-step: how to make gunkan

Red and yellow pepper, onion and mushroom
Prawn, wasabi and cream cheese
Butter grilled scallop
Seaweed, onion and sesame soy sauce
Spicy salmon
Marinated tuna

PARTY PIECES

*Anyone can roll a delicious, satisfying hand roll,
or fill a wonderful gunkan. So invite all your
friends and have a ball!*

Sushi parties

This chapter contains the secrets to some of the best and most memorable dinner parties you will ever throw. Two types of sushi — gunkan (sushi 'battleships'), and hand rolls — are ideal for novices to make. Simply make the sushi rice in advance (see page 20) and, in the case of gunkan, make up a few gunkan bases (see page 64), then lay out a cornucopia of filling ingredients on the table. With just a few simple verbal tips, you can get everyone around the table filling and rolling their own sushi, with their own individual and unexpected combinations... perhaps you'll discover a future classic!

HOW TO MAKE HAND ROLLS

Salmon and avocado

½ sheet of nori seaweed (halved horizontally)
65g prepared sushi rice (see page 20, about the size of a medium egg)
2 cucumber batons
2 salmon strips (see page 25)

157 kcal per roll

Place the seaweed on a work surface, rough side up and shiny side down.

Take the rice and spread it on the left hand side of the seaweed, if you are right-handed. (**Or** simply reverse all the instructions.)

Place the cucumber and salmon diagonally across the middle of the rice, so that they stick out at the top left corner. Pick up the rice-laden sheet of nori in your left hand.

Lift the bottom left corner of the seaweed up over the fillings to make a cone, then lift the right hand side of the seaweed and keep rolling. The nori sheet will stick to itself to seal the roll.

I call these the DIY rolls because you don't need any kit to make them. Each recipe below makes 1 roll, simply scale up to make as many as you want.

HAND ROLLS

For each hand roll, you will need:
½ sheet of nori seaweed (halved horizontally)
65g prepared sushi rice (see page 20, the size of a medium egg)

To make the hand roll, refer to the step-by-step guide (see page 55).

MAKE A WISH

3 okra fingers, blanched in salted water for 2 minutes
pinch of shredded spring onion
½ tsp black sesame seeds (optional)
4 shiso leaves (or see note overleaf)*

134 kcal per roll

MONK ROLL

1½ tbsp grated carrot
1 shiso leaf (or see note overleaf)*
4 chives, cut into 6cm lengths
1 tsp black sesame seeds

128 kcal per roll

FIG SURPRISE

½ fresh fig, very thinly sliced
1 tsp cream cheese
3 very thin slices of unwaxed lemon

140 kcal per roll

HINT OF LIME

1 king scallop, sliced into 5 horizontally
3 very thin slices of organic lime

136 kcal per roll

NEW YORK DREAM

1½ tbsp cream cheese mixed with ½ tsp wasabi paste
(wasabi cream cheese)
20g smoked salmon slices
2 very thin slices of unwaxed lemon
4 chives, cut into 6cm lengths
sprinkling of black and white sesame seeds

217 kcal per roll

SUZU YELLOWTAIL

35g yellowtail, thinly sliced as for nigiri (see page 24)
1 shiso leaf (or see note top right)*
½ tsp black sesame seeds (optional)

202 kcal per roll

* If you can't find shiso leaves, substitute with a few chives and rocket leaves.

HOW TO MARINATE MACKEREL FOR SUSHI

Take as many spankingly fresh mackerel fillets as you need and peel off the parchment-like skin (see page 25). Salt on all sides and leave for 30 minutes.

Rinse off the salt. Place in a shallow non-reactive dish and add rice vinegar to soak, turning to coat the fillets on all sides. Cover and refrigerate overnight. The vinegar will 'cook' the fish. Pat dry to use.

PRAWN HEAVEN

1 piece King Prawn Tempura (see page 40)
3 avocado slices
5g tobiko (flying fish roe, optional)

175 kcal per roll

OMEGA-3 HIT

35g thinly sliced Marinated Mackerel (see above)
4 cucumber batons

223 kcal per roll

HOW TO MAKE GUNKAN

Chopped prawn

12 x 3cm strip of nori seaweed
10–13g prepared sushi rice (see page 20, about the size of a thumb)
2 prawns, chopped

33 kcal per piece

Place the seaweed on a work surface, rough side up and shiny side down.

Wrap the strip of seaweed around the rice, so the rough side faces inwards. The rice should come just halfway up the seaweed case.

Gently press both ends of the seaweed strip together. They should stick to each other to seal. This is the gunkan base.

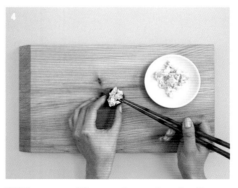

Fill the case with your chosen topping (in this case chopped prawns), and serve.

Gunkan means 'shape of the boat'. They make a really pretty display. Each recipe below makes 5 pieces, simply scale up to make as many as you want.

GUNKAN

For each piece of gunkan, you will need:

12 x 3cm strip of nori seaweed
10–13g prepared sushi rice (the size of a thumb)

To make the gunkan, refer to the step-by-step guide (see left).

RED AND YELLOW PEPPER, ONION AND MUSHROOM

1 tsp vegetable oil
100g yellow pepper, cut into 5mm cubes
100g red pepper, cut into 5mm cubes
100g onion, cut into 5mm cubes
20g mushroom, cut into 5mm cubes

Place a saucepan over a medium heat and add the oil. Add all the vegetables and cook for 5 minutes. Cool down for 10 minutes.

Divide between the gunkan.

48 kcal per piece

PRAWN, WASABI AND CREAM CHEESE

50g cooked prawns (see page 40), chopped
150g cream cheese
2 tbsp wasabi
a few spring onions pieces, very finely chopped, to serve (optional)

In a small bowl, mix the prawns well with the cream cheese and wasabi, cover and leave in the refrigerator for 30 minutes.

Divide between the gunkan and top with the spring onion slivers (if using) to serve.

153 kcal per piece

BUTTER GRILLED SCALLOP

10g unsalted butter
50g scallops, cut into 1cm cubes
1 tsp soy sauce

Melt the butter in a small frying pan over a medium heat.

Add the scallops and cook for 3 minutes, until brown on all sides. Add the soy sauce, turn the scallops to coat, then remove from the pan, cover and marinate for 15 minutes.

Divide between the gunkan.

47 kcal per piece

SEAWEED, ONION AND SESAME SOY SAUCE

4 tbsp dried wakame seaweed
20g finely sliced onion
1 tbsp soy sauce
1 tsp lemon juice
½ tsp white sesame seeds

Place the seaweed and onion in separate bowls, cover with cold water and leave to soak for 15 minutes.

Drain the seaweed and squeeze the water out. Drain the onion and pat dry with kitchen paper. Mix the onion and seaweed in a bowl. Add the soy sauce, lemon juice and sesame seeds and mix well.

Divide between the gunkan.

29 kcal per piece

SPICY SALMON

50g salmon
½ tsp mayonnaise
1 tsp eel sauce (from Asian stores; this is sweet, thick soy sauce)
½ tsp chilli powder (ideally Japanese chilli powder)

Mince the salmon with a sharp knife, place in a small bowl and add the mayonnaise, eel sauce and chilli. Mix well.

Divide between the gunkan.

47 kcal per piece

MARINATED TUNA

50g tuna
1 tsp soy sauce
1 tsp mirin
pinch of finely chopped spring onion (optional)

Slice the tuna into 1cm chunks, place in a small bowl and add the soy sauce and mirin. Stir, cover and leave to marinate for 15 minutes.

Divide between the gunkan. Sprinkle with the spring onion to serve (if using).

36 kcal per piece

Soups and salads

MISO
Tofu and seaweed
Hearty root vegetable
Aubergine
Mackerel
Spicy pork
Spring onion and spinach
Potato and onion
Shiitake mushroom, spinach and onion

SECRETS OF THE JAPANESE POWER BREAKFAST
Japanese omelette
Pickles
Grilled salmon

COLLAGEN SOUPS
Chicken collagen soup
Facelift-in-a-bowl

SALADS
Japanese coleslaw
Steamed vegetables with creamy tofu dressing
Oil-free mushroom salad
Lightly grilled tuna with rocket
Aubergine and shallot salad
Oil-free edamame
No-carb 'wrap wrap wrap'
Fill-you-up soba noodle salad
Tuna and avocado tartare
Popeye spinach salad
Onion and seaweed salad
Steamed sesame chicken salad

MIGHTY MISO

Despite the fact that miso is a thin soup, and very low in calories, drinking it can fill you up disproportionately. Try having a cup with each meal.

Miso soup is a favourite of mine, as you can come up with so many varieties depending on what you have in your storecupboard or fridge. It's nutritious but calorie-light. Here are some of my most popular crowd-pleasers. If you are a vegetarian, simply use a miso paste that does not contain bonito flakes, and omit any other bonito flakes in the recipe.

TO MAKE BASIC MISO SOUP

10–12g miso paste with
bonito flakes

Boil 150ml of water in a saucepan,
then reduce the heat to low. Put the
miso paste on a spoon. Immerse half
of the spoon into the boiling water,
mixing the paste and a small amount
of water together on the spoon to
form a roux. Mix this roux into the
rest of the water in the pan.

Makes 1 bowl
30 kcal per bowl

TOFU AND SEAWEED

Pictured on page 73

1 tsp dried wakame seaweed
1 quantity Basic Miso Soup
20g firm tofu, cut into 1cm cubes

Soak the seaweed in water for
10 minutes, then drain and add
to the miso with the tofu.

Makes 1 bowl
46 kcal per bowl

HEARTY ROOT VEGETABLE

Pictured left

½ tsp bonito flakes
50g mooli, finely sliced
1 small carrot, finely sliced
½ large onion, finely chopped
1 tbsp miso paste

Boil 600ml of water in a saucepan.
Add the bonito flakes and all the
vegetables. Cook them for 3 minutes,
until the vegetables soften. Turn the
heat off.

Add the miso paste to the soup
through a small sieve, using a
teaspoon to push it through.

Turn the heat back on until it boils,
stirring, then serve.

Makes 2 bowls
59 kcal per bowl

AUBERGINE

20g sliced Japanese aubergine
1 quantity Basic Miso Soup

Grill the aubergine for 3 minutes on
each side, then cut into 1cm cubes.
Add to the miso.

Makes 1 bowl
34 kcal per bowl

MACKEREL

20g smoked mackerel, sliced
1 quantity Basic Miso Soup

Add the fish to the soup just long
enough to heat through, then serve.

Makes 1 bowl
70 kcal per bowl

SPICY PORK

20g Spicy Miso Minced Meat with
pork (see page 100)
1 quantity Basic Miso Soup

Add the pork to the soup just long
enough to heat through, then serve.

Makes 1 bowl
100 kcal per bowl

SPRING ONION AND SPINACH

large pinch of shredded spring onion
5 large spinach leaves
1 quantity Basic Miso Soup

Add the spring onion and spinach to
the miso just before serving.

Makes 1 bowl
33 kcal per bowl

POTATO AND ONION

30g potato, cut into 1cm cubes
10–12g miso paste with bonito flakes
a few thin slices of onion

Cook the potato in 150ml of boiling
water until just tender, before adding
the miso. Add the onion to serve.

Makes 1 bowl
55 kcal per bowl

SHIITAKE MUSHROOM, SPINACH AND ONION

20g shiitake mushrooms, sliced
3 large spinach leaves
a few thin slices of onion
10–12g miso paste with bonito flakes

Place the mushrooms, spinach and
onion in 150ml of boiling water for
3 minutes. Add the miso, then serve.

Makes 1 bowl
36 kcal per bowl

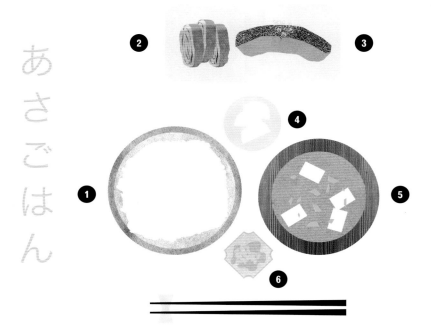

あさごはん

1 100g cooked rice **168 kcal** / **2** 30g Japanese omelette **86 kcal** / **3** 120g grilled salmon **246 kcal**
4 20g Japanese pickles **6 kcal** / **5** 120g miso soup **24 kcal** / **6** 1 tbsp natto **30 kcal**
560 kcal total

Secrets of the Japanese power breakfast

The traditional Japanese breakfast is a hearty feast, a world away from a slice of toast grabbed on the go. A spread of dishes charms the eye and satisfies the tastebuds… though the flavours are a little stronger than those Westerners are used to at breakfast.

If you have made, portioned and frozen the rice and omelette parts of breakfast, and have a jar of Japanese pickles, it will only take five minutes to grill the salmon and make the soup.

You do not have to eat a Japanese breakfast to follow Sushi Slim, so this is here just to show you what you're missing! If you want to try it, but don't have time during the week, give it a go for brunch at the weekend. You will find that you'll struggle to eat later in the day… which is, of course, part of the secret of the enviable Japanese figure.

Natto, a relish of fermented soy beans, can be an acquired taste. We mix it with soy sauce and eat it with rice. Try it; it's addictive.

When sugar is added to the omelette, it is usually used to top or fill sushi; whereas the sugar-free version is used in hot food. Obviously, children prefer the version with sugar!

A Japanese omelette is denser than the Western type and is cut into slices to be chilled for up to three days, or wrapped and frozen, or eaten straight away, as desired.

JAPANESE OMELETTE WITHOUT SUGAR

1½ tsp cornflour
6 free-range eggs
1 tsp salt
1 tbsp sesame oil (optional)

Dissolve the cornflour in 7 tbsp of water in a large bowl. Beat in the eggs with the salt.

Add the sesame oil to a frying pan over a medium heat. (If you use a non-stick pan you won't need the oil.)

Add one ladle's worth of egg mixture to the pan, tilting it until the base is completely covered. Cook until the egg mixture is just about to set.

Fold the egg over on itself three times in 6cm folds. Keep the omelette in the pan, and ladle more egg into the newly made space, lifting the first omelette with a spatula to allow the raw egg to flow underneath.

Once the new egg mixture ia about to set, fold three times again, encasing the first omelette, creating a layered effect. Repeat until the egg mixture has been used up. Serve, or divide into 6, wrap and freeze separately.

Serves 6
516 kcal in total, **86 kcal** per serving

JAPANESE OMELETTE WITH SUGAR

Make as above, but add to the egg mixture:

½ tsp bonito flakes, dissolved in a little water
1 tsp soy sauce
1½ tbsp caster sugar

Serves 6
872 kcal in total, **145 kcal** per serving

JAPANESE PICKLES

You can of course buy these pickles, but this is a very light, salty relish to add pep to your meals. It will store in the fridge for 3 to 5 days.

600–700g head of Chinese leaf or cabbage
1 tbsp sea salt
1 dried chilli
1 garlic clove, finely sliced

Cut the Chinese leaf into quarters and wash it well.

Put it into a non-reactive plastic container and add the salt, chilli and garlic. Mix well, then weight down with a sterilised stone, or a plate with cans of food on top.

Leave for half a day before eating.

Makes enough for 5 family breakfasts
180–210 kcal in total

GRILLED SALMON

One of the healthiest and most common breakfast dishes in Japan. Think of it as an alternative to kippers or kedgeree.

1 tsp sea salt
120g salmon fillet

Sprinkle the salt on to all sides of the salmon and leave it for 20 minutes.

Grill it for 5 minutes, turning once.

Serve.

Serves 1
246 kcal

Beauty departments are now filled with sachets of liquid collagen to add to your beauty routine, but in Japan we incorporate this goodie into our daily diet. The skin-tightening effects are visible even the day after eating.

I give chicken and fish versions of Collagen Soup here and overleaf.

There is a restaurant in Tokyo that I have been to three times where they only serve collagen-rich grouper soup, in large communal bowls. The restaurant is full of women diners, who fight over the extra-rich soup left in the bottom of the bowl, while they are served by the all-male waiting staff.

We are taught that collagen is most easily absorbed by the body when it comes from fish, though it is also absorbed when it comes from poultry. Although red meat contains collagen, we think it is difficult to digest and so does not do the same great job on the skin.

CHICKEN COLLAGEN SOUP

1.5kg medium whole chicken
1 tbsp sea salt
3cm root ginger, sliced, slices
crushed with the back of a knife
1 leek, finely sliced lengthways and
cut into 6cm lengths
1 tsp black pepper

Pour 1 litre of water into a large saucepan and add the chicken, salt and ginger. Bring to the boil over a medium heat, then reduce the heat and simmer for 30 minutes.

Remove the chicken from the pan and remove all the bones and skin. Strain the stock, then return it to the rinsed-out pan. Return the chicken meat to the pan with the leek. Return to a gentle simmer, and cook for another 10 minutes.

Season with black pepper and serve in warmed soup bowls.

If not serving immediately, allow to cool thoroughly at room temperature in a shallow, sealed container, then chill in the fridge. Once it's chilled it takes on a jelly-like quality and you should be able to cut it into 7.5cm cubes (see far left). Pop a couple of these into a flask or sealed cup and simply microwave for 2 minutes for a lunchtime super-beautifying soup. Store the rest in your freezer and use it up within 1 month.

If you like, you can add grated carrot and sliced shiitake mushroom caps to each bowl of soup.

You can also freeze the cubes without chicken meat for a far lower-calorie collagen soup.

Serves 4
1,196 kcal in total, with chicken meat
299 kcal per bowl, with chicken meat

Grouper is full of collagen and, for that reason, it is expensive in Japan and the food of the rich and famous. It is economical in the West, though.

You can of course omit the fish head, but you will lose a lot of collagen if you do. I promise you, it's worth it!

FACELIFT-IN-A-BOWL

1 grouper head, plus 100–120g grouper fillet
½ x 496g packet of firm tofu (optional)
½ leek
20g Chinese leaf, cut into 2cm strips
20g beansprouts
2 fresh shiitake mushrooms, cut into 1cm slices
3 tbsp soy sauce
1cm root ginger, grated
5cm mooli, grated

Put the fish head and 500ml of water in a large pan. Bring slowly to the boil, then reduce the heat, cover and simmer for 15 minutes. Remove and discard the fish head. At this point, you may chill, or freeze, the soup base in cubes, as for Chicken Collagen Soup (see page 79). It will be extremely low in calories in this ungarnished state.

Cut the tofu (if using) into 2cm cubes. Cut the leek into 3cm chunks, then cut these into lengthways strips.

Return the fish stock to the boil, then add the grouper fillet, tofu, leek, Chinese leaf, beansprouts and shiitake mushrooms. Cover and cook over a medium heat for 10 minutes.

Uncover and add the soy sauce, ginger and mooli. Serve immediately in warmed bowls.

Serves 2
420 kcal in total
210 kcal per bowl

This Japanese coleslaw is mayo-free and very refreshing, with the low heat of the mooli adding a mild kick. Use bonito flakes instead of spring onion if you eat fish.

We have become used to roasting vegetables. Steaming them is a much healthier option, and the tofu dressing adds a lush silkiness to this dish.

Western mushroom recipes sometimes taste heavy, as they absorb a lot of oil. This raw, no-oil salad is much lighter, but has a gorgeously dense bite to it.

JAPANESE COLESLAW

200g mooli
100g carrot
2 tbsp soy sauce
2 tbsp sesame oil
2 tbsp rice vinegar
2 tbsp mirin
1 tsp caster sugar
1 tbsp white sesame seeds, crushed in a mortar and pestle
3 tbsp finely chopped spring onion

Finely slice the mooli and carrot (or shred them using a mandoline), then rinse under cold water.

Mix together all the remaining ingredients, except the spring onion, to make a dressing.

Place the vegetables in a bowl and toss with the dressing. Mound the mooli and carrot like a mountain on a large plate, sprinkle with the spring onion and it's ready!

Serves 2 as an accompaniment
450 kcal in total
225 kcal per serving

STEAMED VEGETABLES WITH CREAMY TOFU DRESSING

For the salad
1 red pepper
1 yellow pepper
40g mooli
1 celery stick
1 tsp sesame seeds

For the dressing
120g silken tofu
10 chives
2 tbsp light soy sauce
1 tbsp lemon juice

Cut all the vegetables into bite-sized pieces and steam for 3 minutes. Drain, then cool them down.

Mix all the ingredients for the dressing in the blender and mix it through the vegetables, then serve, sprinkled with the sesame seeds.

Serves 2
222 kcal in total
111 kcal per serving

OIL-FREE MUSHROOM SALAD

4 shiitake mushrooms
2 enoki mushrooms
2 oyster mushrooms
4 closed cup mushrooms
½ tsp sea salt

Cut the hard part of the stems from the shiitake mushrooms, then trim and finely slice all the mushrooms and sprinkle with sea salt.

Lay them all next to each other on a grill pan and cook under a hot grill for 5 minutes, turning to cook all sides.

Eat them as they are, or with Wasabi Dressing (see page 100).

Serves 2 as an accompaniment
15 kcal in total, without dressing
7.5 kcal per serving, without dressing

The Japanese version of a classic combination. I find the freshness of this dish incredibly cleansing and healthy feeling.

A funky raw food recipe, this tastes rich and will fill you up, but is full of fibre and nutrients.

A perfect 30-second fix to add to a bento box, or grab as a quick snack.

LIGHTLY GRILLED TUNA WITH ROCKET

Pictured left

1 tsp sea salt
200g sushi-grade tuna block
100g rocket salad
1 tsp black and white sesame seeds

For the sauce
2 tbsp soy sauce
1 tsp caster sugar
1½ tbsp rice vinegar
1 tsp sesame oil

Sprinkle the salt on all sides of the tuna and leave it for 15 minutes.

Preheat a non-stick pan over the highest heat. When it is very hot, add the tuna. As soon as it colours, turn it to colour on another side. Remove from the pan once it is seared all over. Place on a plate, cover and put in the fridge to cool rapidly for 15 minutes.

Mix together all the ingredients for the sauce.

Slice the tuna into wafer-thin slices, place it on a plate with the rocket, drizzle with the sauce and scatter with the sesame seeds, serving any remaining sauce on the side.

Serves 2
328 kcal in total
164 kcal per serving

AUBERGINE AND SHALLOT SALAD

400g Japanese aubergine
2 tbsp sea salt
4 shallots, finely sliced
1 tbsp sesame oil
1 tbsp light soy sauce
½ tbsp lemon juice
1 tsp white sesame seeds, crushed in a mortar and pestle
5 chives, finely chopped

Cut the aubergine into 1.5cm slices. Place in a bowl and sprinkle with the salt. Rub it through the slices for at least 3 minutes, then rinse and pat the slices dry with kitchen paper.

Place in a bowl and add the shallots, then sprinkle the other ingredients on top, toss and serve.

Serves 2 as an accompaniment
312 kcal in total
156 kcal per serving

OIL-FREE EDAMAME

250g frozen edamame beans
½ tsp sea salt

Defrost the beans, then sprinkle with the salt.

Serves 2 as an accompaniment
398 kcal in total
199 kcal per serving

An indulgent dish, but very low in carbohydrate. Without realising it you will be eating a lot of greens here, while enjoying a heady hit of umami, the irresistible savoury flavour.

NO CARB 'WRAP WRAP WRAP'

250g beef fillet

For the marinade
1 tbsp soy sauce
thin wedge of eating apple, finely grated
½ tsp finely grated garlic
1 tsp finely grated root ginger
½ tbsp chilli powder (ideally Japanese chilli powder)
1 tsp English mustard powder
1 tbsp sesame oil

For the salad
1 round lettuce, washed, leaves separated
20g mooli, shredded
1 cucumber, sliced into batons
2 garlic cloves, finely sliced

Put the beef in the freezer for 1 hour to firm up (but make sure you don't forget about it: you don't want it to freeze). This will make it easier to slice thinly. Slice the beef as thinly as you can.

Mix all the marinade ingredients in a bowl, add the beef and mix well. Cover and leave to marinate for 20 minutes. Preheat a grill. Grill the beef for 2 or 3 minutes on each side.

To assemble the wrap, hold a lettuce leaf in your hand, add some mooli and cucumber, then some beef and garlic. Wrap the lettuce leaf around and eat.

Serves 2
566 kcal in total
283 kcal per serving

A great recipe to keep hunger at bay, light but incredibly tasty. I find this salad quite addictive. You can make more noodles than you need, then wrap portions individually and freeze them. Defrost under running water. Don't be tempted to defrost them in a microwave, as this will soften their texture.

FILL-YOU-UP SOBA NOODLE SALAD

For the salad
200g soba noodles
240g baby spinach leaves
handful of cherry tomatoes (optional)

For the dressing
4 tbsp sesame oil
6 tbsp soy sauce
2 tbsp lemon juice
2 tbsp white sesame seeds, crushed in a mortar and pestle, plus more to serve
2 tsp chilli powder (ideally Japanese chilli powder)

Bring 4 litres of water to a boil and cook the soba noodles for 15 minutes (or according to the packet instructions). Drain, then rinse the noodles under cold water. Drain really well once more.

Mix together all the ingredients for the dressing.

Put the noodles, spinach and tomatoes (if using) in a bowl, toss with the dressing, sprinkle with sesame seeds and serve.

Serves 2
1,002 kcal in total
501 kcal per serving

A tuna dish with an incredibly luxurious texture, this is a really healthy but indulgent treat.

Spinach and sesame salad is a must-eat in Japan. We keep it in the fridge to eat daily.

This is incredibly refreshing and clean tasting. I would eat it every day if I could.

TUNA AND AVOCADO TARTARE

For the onion dressing
1 onion, roughly chopped
1 tbsp clear honey
1 tbsp sushi vinegar
1 tbsp grapeseed oil
¼ tsp sea salt
¼ tsp black pepper
½ tbsp dill, finely chopped

For the tartare
50g sushi-grade tuna loin
½ avocado

Blitz all the ingredients for the onion dressing in a blender until smooth.

With a sharp knife, finely mince the tuna. Now you can go 2 ways: either slice the avocado and place the slices on a mound of tuna, or mash the avocado to a smooth paste and mix it in with the minced tuna.

Serve it with the onion dressing, and with wasabi paste for dipping.

Serves 2
456 kcal in total
228 kcal per serving

POPEYE SPINACH SALAD

250g frozen spinach
½ tbsp white sesame seeds, crushed in a mortar and pestle
½ tbsp soy sauce
1 tsp caster sugar
½ tbsp sesame oil

Put the spinach in a saucepan and add just enough water to cover. Bring to a boil, reduce the heat and simmer until the spinach has defrosted. Drain and, when cool enough to handle, squeeze out all the water.

Put the spinach in a bowl and mix in the remaining ingredients. Toss and serve.

Serves 2 as an accompaniment
184 kcal in total
92 kcal per serving

ONION AND SEAWEED SALAD

2 tbsp dried wakame seaweed
1 onion, finely sliced
2 tbsp lemon juice
1 tbsp light soy sauce
1 tbsp mirin

Soak the seaweed and onion separately in water for 15 minutes, then drain. Squeeze the excess water from the seaweed, and pat the onion dry on kitchen paper. Place both into a bowl.

Add the lemon juice, soy sauce and mirin and mix well.

Serves 2 as an accompaniment
138 kcal in total
69 kcal per serving

This is my family's favourite salad; it's filling, tasty but incredibly healthy.

STEAMED SESAME CHICKEN SALAD

For the dressing
4 tbsp soy sauce
4 tbsp caster sugar
3 tbsp rice vinegar
½ cube chicken stock
½ tsp sea salt
1 tbsp sesame oil

For the salad
1 tsp sea salt
1 chicken breast
2 tbsp sake
½ medium Iceberg lettuce, thinly sliced
½ cucumber, thinly sliced
a few wedges of tomato
a few thin slices of red onion

Put everything for the dressing except the sesame oil into a saucepan with 8 tbsp of water. Place over a low heat and bring to the boil. Stir, making sure both the sugar and chicken stock cube completely dissolve. Remove from the heat, let cool, then add the sesame oil, cover and chill in the fridge until needed.

Sprinkle the salt on the chicken on both sides and place on a heatproof dish. Add the sake.

Put 2cm of cold water in a large saucepan and add a trivet that emerges above the level of the water. Place the chicken dish on the trivet. Cover the saucepan.

Place the saucepan on the hob and cook on a medium heat for 25 minutes from start to finish.

Remove the dish from the saucepan, and leave until cool enough to handle. Tear the chicken into strips.

Put the lettuce on a plate and arrange the cucumber, tomato and red onion over. Put the chicken on top. Toss with the sesame dressing and serve.

Serves 2
494 kcal in total
247 kcal per serving

Beautiful bentos

The ultimate lunch box

NO. 1
Mighty meat

NO. 2
Stuffed peppers and rice balls

NO. 3
Chicken teriyaki

NO. 4
Low-fat protein punch

NO. 5
Sweet chilli prawns

NO. 6
Spicy chicken-and-egg

NO. 7
California rolls

NO. 8
Salad day

NO. 9
Omega-3 and wasabi veg

NO. 10
California rolls with protein boost

MAKE YOUR BOSS JEALOUS!

All the constituent parts of each bento can be made at the weekend, wrapped and frozen in portions. Aim for lots of different colours in a bento, for maximum nutrition.

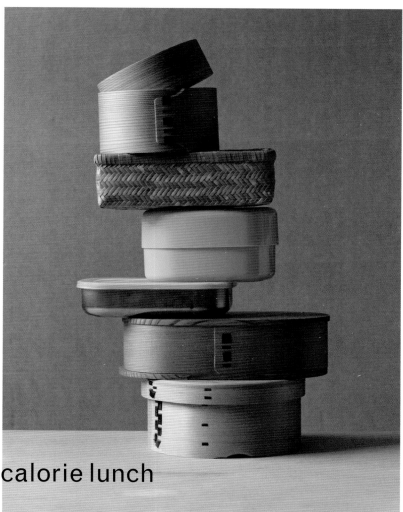

The 500-calorie lunch

Lunch can be a dangerous time when you are watching what you eat. But what if you could take to work a feast; a whole panoply of delicious dishes wrapped up in a beautiful box, safe in the knowledge that someone else has counted the calories for you? Well, now you can.

Here are 10 bento boxes, one for every working day of two weeks, each of which contains around 500 calories. Every recipe can be made in a trice at the weekend, wrapped and frozen in portions. On a working morning, it's simply a case of packing your selection of dishes from the freezer. By lunch time, your food will be perfectly defrosted. You can mix and match the components of the bento boxes that follow, just bear in mind that this may tip the calorie count to more than 500.

You'll be the envy of your workmates, eating a healthier, more satisfying option than a mayo-laden sandwich. I tend to follow a rough rule of one-half rice, one-quarter vegetables and one-quarter protein in a bento box, and you can include Miso or Collagen Soups (see pages 74–75 and 78–81) in winter.

キレイなお弁当

NO. 1
Mighty meat

TOFU STEAK
SPICY MISO MINCED MEAT
MIXED SEAWEED WITH OKRA
WHITE RICE

507 kcal

NO. 2
Stuffed peppers and rice balls

STUFFED GREEN PEPPERS WITH TURKEY
ONIGIRI
GRILLED PUMPKIN
FRESH TOMATOES

501 kcal

NO. 3
Chicken teriyaki

CHICKEN TERIYAKI
EDAMAME RICE
GREEN BEANS AND ALMOND BUTTER
CREAMY PUMPKIN

495 kcal

NO. 4
Low-fat protein punch

GRILLED SALMON
JAPANESE OMELETTE WITH CHIVES
OIL-FREE MUSHROOM SALAD
POPEYE SPINACH SALAD
BROWN RICE

509 kcal

NO. 5
Sweet chilli prawns

SWEET CHILLI PRAWNS
JAPANESE OMELETTE WITH EDAMAME OR GREEN PEA
ASPARAGUS WITH MUSHROOMS AND SESAME OIL
BROWN RICE

500 kcal

キレイなお弁当

NO. 6

Spicy chicken-and-egg

**SPICY CHICKEN
BOILED ASPARAGUS
BALSAMIC PICKLED EGG
BROWN RICE**

504 kcal

NO. 7

California rolls

**JAPANESE OMELETTE, BEAN
AND CRAB CALIFORNIA ROLL
OIL-FREE EDAMAME**

482 kcal

NO. 8

Salad day

**FILL-YOU-UP SOBA NOODLE
SALAD**

501 kcal

NO. 9

Omega-3 and wasabi veg

**SMOKED MACKEREL
JAPANESE OMELETTE WITH
EDAMAME OR GREEN PEA
MIXED VEGETABLES WITH
WASABI DRESSING
WHITE RICE**

459 kcal

NO. 10

California rolls with
protein boost

**SMOKED SALMON AND
CUCUMBER CALIFORNIA ROLL
JAPANESE OMELETTE
OIL-FREE EDAMAME**

489 kcal

キレイなお弁当

NO. 1
Mighty meat

For days when you fancy a bit more protein.

TOFU STEAK

If you are craving a meaty texture, switch to this dish. It's bursting with vegetable proteins that are easy to digest.

For the tofu steak
550g firm tofu
1 tsp sea salt
10g finely grated root ginger
3 tbsp cornflour
5 tbsp cooking oil

For the wasabi dressing
2 tbsp soy sauce
½ tbsp wasabi paste
1 tsp grapeseed oil

Place a few layers of kitchen paper on a plate. Remove the tofu from the packet and put it on the kitchen paper. Leave for 20 minutes, to remove all the moisture. Cut into 3cm squares and place in a bowl. Add the sea salt and ginger and sprinkle with the cornflour. Turn to coat on all sides.

Heat a pan over a medium heat and add the cooking oil. Add the tofu to the pan and brown on all sides.

Meanwhile, mix all the ingredients for the dressing in a small bowl. Mix the tofu steaks with the wasabi dressing and serve. Or divide into 8 portions, wrap and freeze separately. Use 1 portion for a bento box.

Makes 8 bento box portions
1,056 kcal in total
132 kcal per serving

SPICY MISO MINCED MEAT

An Asian twist on a mince dish.

¾ tbsp cooking oil
95g finely chopped spring onion
15g finely grated root ginger
15g finely chopped garlic
265g minced pork or turkey
1¼ tbsp caster sugar
1¾ tbsp miso paste
3 tbsp soy sauce
2½ tbsp sake
¾ chicken stock cube
1¼ tsp tobanjan (chilli bean sauce, optional)

Heat the oil in a frying pan over a low heat. Add the spring onion, ginger and garlic and stir well until softened.

Add the minced meat, increase the heat to medium and cook until lightly brown. Add all the other ingredients except the tobanjan with 2 tbsp of water, stir, and cook for 5 minutes, or until all the liquid has evaporated.

Add the tobanjan (if using), and serve. Or divide into 4 portions, wrap and freeze separately. Use 1 portion for a bento box.

Makes 4 bento box portions
with turkey **536 kcal** in total;
with pork **928 kcal** in total
with turkey **134 kcal** per serving;
with pork **232** per serving

MIXED SEAWEED WITH OKRA

Bursting with vitamins and minerals that all add beauty and health benefits to this gorgeous side dish.

8 fingers of okra
½ tsp salt
8 tbsp mixed edible seaweed
4 tbsp soy sauce
4 tbsp lime juice

Add the okra and salt to boiling water for 1 minute. Drain, and chop finely. Put the seaweed in a bowl, cover with warm water and soak for 10 minutes. Drain and squeeze out the water.

Mix the okra, seaweed, soy sauce and lime juice. Serve, or divide into 4 portions, wrap and freeze separately. Use 1 portion for a bento box.

Makes 4 bento box portions
108 kcal in total
27 kcal per serving

WHITE RICE

Add 165g cooked Japanese white rice (see page 20) to this bento box.

Makes 1 bento box portion
214 kcal per serving

NO. 2
Stuffed peppers and rice balls

Simple to prepare, but very impressive!

STUFFED GREEN PEPPERS WITH TURKEY

Make extra of this at supper for tomorrow's bento box. Delicious.

120g finely chopped onion
1 tsp cooking oil, for the onion, plus 1 tbsp for the peppers
480g minced turkey
salt, to taste
1 egg, beaten
4 small green peppers
4 tsp plain flour
4 tbsp balsamic vinegar
2 tbsp mirin

Cook the onion over a medium heat with the 1 tsp of oil until soft. Tip into a bowl. Add the turkey, salt and egg and mix well. Leave for 20 minutes.

Cut each pepper in half and remove the seeds and ribs. Fill each half with the turkey mixture, and sprinkle the turkey with the flour.

Add the 1 tbsp of oil to a frying pan over a medium heat. Add the peppers, turkey-side down. Cook for 3 minutes. Turn and cook for another 3 minutes.

Add the balsamic vinegar and mirin, cover and cook for a final 5 minutes, or until the pepper has softened and the stuffing is cooked through. Serve, or divide into 4 portions, wrap and freeze separately. Use 1 portion for a bento box.

Makes 4 bento box portions
1,146 kcal in total
287 kcal per serving

ONIGIRI

Traditional Japanese rice balls are an easy low-calorie lunch time snack, great for when you need a carb hit.

400g hot, cooked Japanese white rice (see page 20)
salt
4 thick strips of nori seaweed

Take one-quarter of the rice and mould it into a ball in your hands.

Sprinkle salt all over the rice and pat it in firmly, then wrap the seaweed around the rice and it's ready to eat! Repeat to use all the rice and seaweed. If making in advance, wrap and freeze each onigiri separately. Use 1 onigiri in a bento box.

Makes 4 bento box portions
683 kcal in total
171 kcal per serving

GRILLED PUMPKIN

Couldn't be simpler. Grilling gives pumpkin a real sweetness for when you need a sugary-but-healthy fix.

240g green-skinned pumpkin
salt

Cut the pumpkin into 5mm-thick slices. Lay them on a grill pan and cook under a hot grill for 5 minutes, turning to cook both sides. You should get speckles of black.

Sprinkle salt all over the pumpkin. Serve, or divide into 4 portions, wrap and freeze separately. Use 1 portion for a bento box.

Makes 4 bento box portions
116 kcal in total
29 kcal per serving

FRESH TOMATOES

Add 3 fresh cherry tomatoes to each bento box.

14 kcal per serving

Most Westerners know this dish. Popular the world over for its sweet-salty tastiness, it contains plenty of garlic and ginger.

CHICKEN TERIYAKI

4 skinless chicken breasts
(each 100g)
4 tsp vegetable oil

For the sauce
2 tbsp soy sauce
4 tsp mirin
2 tbsp sake
2 tbsp caster sugar
2 tbsp rice vinegar
2 tbsp finely grated root ginger
2 tbsp finely grated garlic
2 dried chillies, finely chopped

Mix together all the ingredients for the sauce in a non-reactive shallow dish. Place the chicken in the sauce, turn to coat all over, cover and leave to marinate in the fridge for up to 1 hour.

Add the oil to a frying pan over a medium heat. Once the oil is hot, add the chicken and fry on each side for 4 minutes, or until cooked through, then add all the marinade and bubble up until it is sticky and reduced. Serve, or divide into 4 portions, wrap and freeze separately. Use 1 portion for a bento box.

Makes 4 bento box portions
776 kcal in total
194 kcal per serving

Chicken teriyaki

The pulses and vegetables in this bento box add bulk without heavy carbs or fats.

CHICKEN TERIYAKI

→ See left

EDAMAME RICE

480g hot, cooked Japanese white rice (see page 20)
40–60g shelled edamame beans

Mix the rice with the edamame. Serve, or divide into 4 portions, wrap and freeze separately. Use 1 portion for a bento box.

Makes 4 bento box portions
904 kcal in total
226 kcal per serving

GREEN BEANS AND ALMOND BUTTER

I like to use almond butter to bring out the flavour of the beans.

4 tsp almond butter
large pinch of caster sugar
1 tsp miso paste
salt
160g green beans, trimmed

Mix the almond butter in a bowl with the sugar, miso and salt to taste.

Bring a saucepan of water to a boil and add salt. Drop in the beans and cook for 3 minutes, until soft.

Drain the beans, toss them in the bowl with the almond mixture and mix well.

Serve, or divide into 4 portions, wrap and freeze separately. Use 1 portion for a bento box.

Makes 4 bento box portions
152 kcal in total
38 kcal per serving

CREAMY PUMPKIN

A healthy but beautifully rich-tasting dish. Filling and great for you.

160g green-skinned pumpkin
2 tsp sake
2 tsp caster sugar
2 tsp mirin
2 tsp soy sauce

Remove all the seeds from the pumpkin and cut the flesh into 3cm pieces.

Put it in a pan with 400ml of water and the remaining ingredients, making sure the pumpkin skin is touching the base of the pan. Cover the saucepan and bring to a boil over a high heat. Reduce the heat and simmer for 15 minutes.

Remove the lid and cook over a medium heat until all the water has evaporated. Serve, or divide into 4 portions, wrap and freeze separately. Use 1 portion for a bento box.

Makes 4 bento box portions
148 kcal in total
37 kcal per serving

キレイなお弁当

NO. 4
Low-fat protein punch

High in protein, this bento box will fill you up all day.

GRILLED SALMON

→ See page 77, Use ½ x quantity Grilled Salmon (60g). Use one-half the quantity of salmon you would serve for a Japanese breakfast as a bento box portion.

Makes 1 bento box portion
123 kcal per serving

JAPANESE OMELETTE WITH CHIVES

→ See page 77. Make the omelette with a generous handful of finely chopped chives. Use 1 serving as a bento box portion.

Makes 1 bento box portion
86 kcal per serving

OIL-FREE MUSHROOM SALAD

→ See page 83. Use 1 serving as a bento box portion.

Makes 1 bento box portion
7.5 kcal per serving

POPEYE SPINACH SALAD

→ See page 89; use 1 serving as a bento box portion

Makes 1 bento box portion
92 kcal per serving

BROWN RICE

→ See page 20. Add 180g cooked Japanese brown rice to this bento box.

Makes 1 bento box portion
200 kcal per serving

NO. 5
Sweet chilli prawns

Create a lunch time treat with more exotic ingredients to wake up your taste buds.

SWEET CHILLI PRAWNS

Guaranteed to tick all your taste cravings.

280g raw prawns, deveined

For the marinade
1 tsp salt
4 tsp sake
4 tsp cornflour
1½ tsp sesame oil

For the rest
4 tbsp tomato ketchup
4 tsp miso paste
4 tsp caster sugar
2 tsp finely grated root ginger
2 tsp finely grated garlic
2 tsp cooking oil
120g finely chopped spring onion
1 tsp tobanjan (chilli bean sauce, optional)

Place the prawns in a bowl with all the ingredients for the marinade and mix well.

Mix the tomato ketchup, miso, sugar, ginger and garlic in another small bowl with 100ml of water.

Add the oil to a frying pan over a medium heat. Add the spring onion and stir well until you can smell it. Add the prawns and cook, turning, until they are all nice and pink.

Add the ketchup mixture and cook for 3 minutes. Add the tobanjan (if using) and serve. Or divide into 4 portions, wrap and freeze separately (do *not* re-freeze prawns that were previously frozen). Use 1 portion for a bento box.

Makes 4 bento box portions
632 kcal in total
158 kcal per serving

BROWN RICE

→ See page 20. Add 170g cooked Japanese brown rice to this bento box.

Makes 1 bento box portion
191 kcal per serving

ASPARAGUS WITH MUSHROOMS AND SESAME OIL

A really light side dish. The sesame oil gives it an unusual depth.

320g asparagus spears
salt
4 tsp sesame oil
40g mushrooms, finely sliced

Cut the asparagus into 2cm pieces. Cook in boiling salted water for 3 minutes. Drain.

Add the sesame oil to a frying pan over a medium heat. Add the asparagus and mushrooms and stir for 3 minutes, or until the mushrooms are soft. Serve, or divide into 4 portions, wrap and freeze separately.

Makes 4 bento box portions
224 kcal in total
56 kcal per serving

JAPANESE OMELETTE WITH EDAMAME OR GREEN PEA

→ See page 77. Make the omelette with 60g edamame beans, or peas. Use 1 serving as a bento box portion.

Makes 1 bento box portion
95 kcal per serving

NO. 6
Spicy chicken-and-egg

A great bento for days when you want a treat.

SPICY CHICKEN

If you like heat, this does the trick.

2 tbsp English mustard
2 tsp wholegrain mustard
2 tsp white wine vinegar
2 tsp plain flour
4 tsp paprika
4 skinless chicken thighs (80g each)
salt
freshly ground black pepper
2 tsp cooking oil

Mix the 2 mustards, vinegar, flour and paprika in a bowl. Stab the chicken with a fork all over and season. Paint the mustard sauce over the chicken, cover and marinate for 30 minutes.

Put a frying pan over a low heat with the oil. Add the chicken, cover and cook for 10 minutes, turning once. Serve, or divide into 4 portions, wrap and freeze separately.

Makes 4 bento box portions
652 kcal in total
163 kcal per serving

BOILED ASPARAGUS

320g trimmed asparagus spears
salt

Cook the asparagus in boiling salted water for 3 minutes, then drain. Serve, or divide into 4 portions, wrap and freeze separately.

Makes 4 bento box portions
72 kcal in total
18 kcal per serving

BALSAMIC PICKLED EGG

This pickled egg is simple to make and is a great protein snack.

4 eggs
4 tbsp balsamic vinegar
4 tsp soy sauce
2 tsp mirin
2½ tbsp caster sugar

Boil the eggs for 7–8 minutes. The yolk should remain moist. Peel.

Mix the balsamic, soy, mirin and sugar in a saucepan. Heat gently, stirring, until the sugar dissolves.

Put the eggs in a sterilised jar and pour over the hot vinegar. Seal, leave to cool, then refrigerate for 2 days, turning twice a day, before serving.

Makes 4 bento box portions
492 kcal in total
123 kcal per serving

BROWN RICE

→ See page 20. Add 180g cooked Japanese brown rice to this bento box.

Makes 1 bento box portion
200 kcal per serving

キレイなお弁当

NO. 7
California rolls

A soothing combination of calming green goodies and nurturing fish and egg.

SUSHI (FROZEN SUSHI)

→ Take the sushi rolls from your freezer in the morning, pack them in your bento box, and they will be perfectly defrosted by lunchtime.

JAPANESE OMELETTE, BEAN AND CRAB CALIFORNIA ROLL

→ To make the California rolls, refer to the step-by-step guide (see page 36). Fill with:

20g Japanese omelette (see page 77)
10g Green Beans and Almond Butter (see page 103)
2 crab sticks

Makes 1 roll (6 pieces)
382 kcal

OIL-FREE EDAMAME

→ See page 85; add ½ portion to this bento box.

Makes 1 bento box portion
100 kcal per serving

NO. 8
Salad day

The perfect salad combo bento box for when you want fresh, fresh, fresh! This does what it says on the tin and satisfies when you really need to fill up. You can cook the noodles the night before, then add the salad ingredients in the morning. (Or even defrost frozen noodles, see page 87.)

FILL-YOU-UP SOBA NOODLE SALAD

→ See page 87; use 1 serving as a bento box portion

Makes 1 bento box portion
501 kcal per serving

NO. 9
Omega-3 and wasabi veg

A lean and healthy bento, bursting with vitality-boosting ingredients.

SMOKED MACKEREL

50g smoked mackerel, flaked or left whole

130 kcal per serving

JAPANESE OMELETTE WITH EDAMAME OR GREEN PEA

→ See page 77. Make the omelette with 60g of edamame beans, or peas. Use 1 serving as a bento box portion.

Makes 1 bento box portion
95 kcal per serving

MIXED VEGETABLES WITH WASABI DRESSING

8 okra fingers
20 green beans, halved
40g carrot, cut into batons
1 tbsp Wasabi Dressing (see page 100)

Boil the okra, green beans and carrot for 2 minutes, then drain and mix with the Wasabi Dressing. Serve, or divide into 4 portions, wrap and freeze separately.

Makes 4 bento box portions
80 kcal in total
20 kcal per serving

WHITE RICE

Add 165g cooked Japanese white rice (see page 20) to this bento box.

Makes 1 bento box portion
214 kcal per serving

NO. 10
California rolls with protein boost

A selection of classic Japanese goodies, to make you the envy of your work colleagues.

SMOKED SALMON AND CUCUMBER CALIFORNIA ROLL

→ To make the California rolls, refer to the step-by-step guide (see page 36). Fill with:

For the covering
3–4 smoked salmon slices
6 very fine slices of unwaxed lemon

For the filling
2 cucumber batons

Makes 1 roll (6 pieces)
353 kcal

JAPANESE OMELETTE

→ See page 77. Use 1 serving as a bento box portion.

Makes 1 bento box portion
86 kcal per serving

OIL-FREE EDAMAME

→ See page 85; add $\frac{1}{4}$ portion to this bento box.

Makes 1 bento box portion
50 kcal per serving

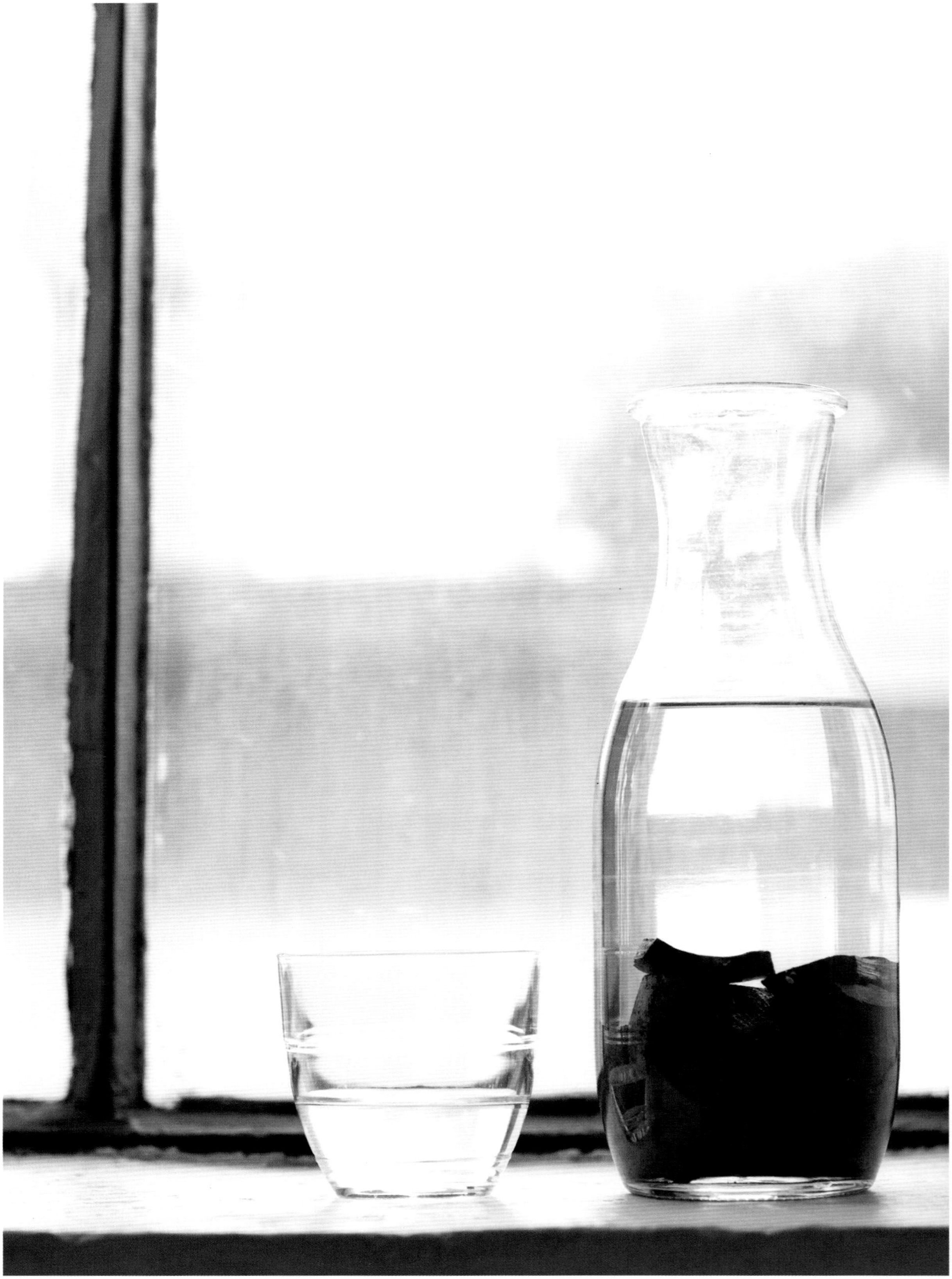

Sushi to impress

Chess sushi
Spring garden
Soba sushi
Treasure in a box
Maki in Spain
Octopus 'tacos'

KAISENDON
Seafood special
Tuna medley
Omega-3 bomb
Salmon lover

ELEGANT, STUNNING SPREADS

These dishes are for special people and magical nights.
Unlike the other recipes in Sushi Slim, you may have to
visit a Japanese store for some of the ingredients.

Visually stunning and inviting, these sushi spreads are an explosion of colour and texture combined with seductive flavours. As you will see in the coming pages, the recipes in this chapter truly pack a huge visual punch, and are perfect for serving at more formal occasions, or when you want to make a big impact. The beautiful sushi tableaux create a party atmosphere. Once made, you can lay them out at the last moment, then you won't have to spend any time in the kitchen away from your guests.

These recipes are not part of the weekly Sushi Slim plan; they are special occasion meals, so I have not included a calorie count. (Though they're healthy and not fattening.) After all, we have to relax every now and then...

Take this idea as a template and let your imagination run wild. You can make your chess board as big as you want, and you can make it with nigiri and gunkan as well as with hosomaki rolls, but it looks best when you use just one type of sushi.

The finest ingredients set the mood for a special evening or celebration. This sushi gets its name from the flower-style shapes it creates. As always, all the fish needs to be sushi-grade. We eat this in springtime, to celebrate the season.

A rice-free roll stuffed instead with buckwheat noodles. Unusual, filling and tasty.

CHESS SUSHI
Pictured left

Four types:
cucumber
avocado and chilli
salmon
tuna

To make the hosomaki rolls, refer to the step-by-step guide (see page 31), using the fillings on pages 32–35.

Serve with soy sauce, pickled ginger and wasabi paste.

Makes as much as you want

SPRING GARDEN
Pictured on page 114

For the yellowtail 'flower'
100g skinned yellowtail fillet
1 shiso leaf, or rocket leaf

For the salmon 'flower'
100g skinned salmon fillet
1 king scallop
1 shiso leaf, or rocket leaf

For the scallop 'flower'
2 king scallops
1 tbsp salmon roe

Cut the yellowtail and salmon into very fine slices on the diagonal, against the grain. Slice the king scallops for the scallop 'flower' 5 times horizontally. Cut the scallop for the salmon 'flower' into strips.

Put a shiso leaf on 2 of 3 plates. Arrange the yellowtail and salmon slices on the plates into flower shapes, treating each slice as a petal, wrapping them around each other. Fill the salmon 'flower' with scallop strips.

Arrange the scallop slices on the third plate as the petals of a flower, placing the salmon roe in the middle.

Serve with soy sauce, pickled ginger and wasabi paste.

Each 'flower' serves 1

SOBA SUSHI
Pictured on page 115

30g soba noodles (cooked weight)
3 tbsp Tempura Sauce
(see page 40)
½ sheet of nori seaweed
(halved horizontally)

Bring 4 litres of water to a boil and cook the soba noodles for 15 minutes (or according to the packet instructions). Drain, then rinse the noodles under cold water. Drain really well once more.

Dress the noodles with the Tempura Sauce, tossing them to coat.

To make the hosomaki rolls, refer to the step-by-step guide (see page 31). Line the noodles up along 1 long side of the nori, straightening them out as far as possible. Cut the roll evenly into 6 pieces, wiping the knife blade between cuts.

Serve with soy sauce, pickled ginger and wasabi paste.

Makes 6 pieces

Sushi to impress

Show your artistic flair with these little Japanese-style wraps.

The addition of air-dried ham to these rolls, using it in place of nori seaweed, gives an unexpected and toothsome twist.

These are little mouthfuls of spiciness.

TREASURE IN A BOX
Pictured left

For the egg crêpe
2 eggs, beaten
½ tsp caster sugar
pinch of salt
¼ tsp flavourless oil

For the filling
10g skinless salmon fillet
5g green beans, trimmed
20g cucumber, deseeded
20g avocado, peeled and stoned
20g bamboo shoot, trimmed
20g shiitake mushrooms, trimmed
70g prepared and seasoned sushi rice (see page 20)

To finish
4 cooked prawns (see page 40), halved lengthways
8 x 6cm lengths of chive

Mix together the eggs, sugar and salt, and heat the oil in a 30cm frying pan. Add the egg batter and swirl the pan to coat the base. When it has set, flip the crêpe and cook the other side for 30 seconds. Remove from the pan.

For the filling, cut everything except the rice into 5mm cubes. Mix them evenly through the rice.

Cut the crêpe into 4 quarter circles. Place one-quarter of the rice mixture in the centre of each piece of crêpe. Wrap as you would a present, to enclose the filling in a neat box.

Arrange on a platter, adding 2 prawn halves and 2 chive lengths to each.

Makes 4 pieces

MAKI IN SPAIN
Pictured on page 118

20g sliced Serrano ham
2 avocado slices
2–3 shiso leaves, or rocket leaves
5 chives
130g prepared and seasoned sushi rice (see page 20)

To make the rolls, refer to the step-by-step guide for hosomaki (see page 31), using ham in place of nori seaweed, and the avocado, shiso and chives as the filling.

Makes 6 pieces

OCTOPUS 'TACOS'
Pictured on page 119

2 tbsp plain flour
1 tbsp chilli powder, ideally Japanese chilli powder
½ tbsp sea salt
40g octopus, cut into 1.5cm chunks
sunflower oil, to deep-fry
4 lettuce leaves
wafer-thin cucumber slices and shredded spring onion, to serve

Mix the flour, chilli powder and salt in a shallow dish. Add the octopus chunks and toss to coat well. Cover and set aside for 30 minutes, for the flavours to get to know each other.

Heat the sunflower oil in a deep, heavy-based saucepan until it reaches 180°C on an oil thermometer.

Fry the pieces of octopus, being careful not to crowd the pan, for 3–4 minutes, turning once, until nicely golden brown. Remove with a slotted spoon and drain briefly on kitchen paper, to remove excess oil.

Lay the lettuce leaves on a platter and scatter a few slices of cucumber into each. Divide the octopus between the lettuce cups, and sprinkle each with spring onion. Serve immediately.

Makes 4 tacos

KAISENDON

Dishes of sashimi laid over seasoned sushi rice, this is opulent special occasion food, and worth a trip to a Japanese shop. As ever, all the fish needs to be sushi-grade.

A stunning, simple yet extravagant dish to share with friends. See page 24 for how to cut fish for sashimi.

One for the connoisseur, this contrasts slices of tuna from different parts of the fish, each prized for its unique qualities.

SEAFOOD SPECIAL
Pictured left, below

250g just-prepared seasoned sushi rice (see page 20)
2 cooked prawns (see page 40)
4 sashimi slices sea bream
4 sashimi slices tuna
4 sashimi slices salmon
4 sashimi slices yellowtail
4 sashimi slices surf clam
1 shiso leaf, or rocket leaf

Spoon the rice into an attractive bowl. It should still have a breath of warmth to it.

Lay on the prawns and the fish, grouping the same type together and arranging them in a circular pattern on the rice. Add the shiso leaf.

Serve with soy sauce, pickled ginger and wasabi paste. Sake makes an excellent accompanying drink.

Serves 1 generously

TUNA MEDLEY
Pictured left, above

250g just-prepared seasoned sushi rice (see page 20)
6 sashimi slices tuna loin (maguro)
4 sashimi slices medium-fatty tuna (chutoro)
3 sashimi slices fatty tuna (otoro)
2 shiso leaves, or rocket leaves

Spoon the rice into an attractive bowl. It should still have a breath of warmth to it.

Lay on the slices of tuna, keeping the same type together and arranging them in lines. Add the shiso leaves, using them to separate each type of tuna.

Serve with soy sauce, pickled ginger and wasabi paste. Eat it with sake or shochu.

Serves 1 generously

An impressive way to prepare and present home-marinated fish at the table.

Salmon tends to be everyone's favourite sushi and sashimi fish, so this is a good choice to serve to sushi novices.

OMEGA-3 BOMB
Pictured right, below

250g just-prepared seasoned sushi rice (see page 20)
2 fillets Marinated Mackerel (see page 59)
1 shiso leaf, or rocket leaf
4 small slices surf clam (optional)

Spoon the rice into an attractive bowl. It should still have a breath of warmth to it.

Cut the mackerel into neat slices and lay it over the rice, retaining the shape of the fillets as far as possible. Arrange the shiso leaf and surf clam (if using) together, over the fish.

Serve with soy sauce, pickled ginger and wasabi paste. Sake makes an excellent accompanying drink.

Serves 1 generously

SALMON LOVER
Pictured right, above

250g just-prepared seasoned sushi rice (see page 20)
12 sashimi slices salmon
1 king scallop
1 tbsp salmon roe

Spoon the rice into an attractive bowl. It should still have a breath of warmth to it.

Lay the salmon over the rice in a circular pattern. Slice the scallop horizontally 5 times, and arrange the slices in the centre of the bowl. Top with the salmon roe.

Serve with soy sauce, pickled ginger and wasabi paste. Eat it with sake or shochu.

Serves 1 generously

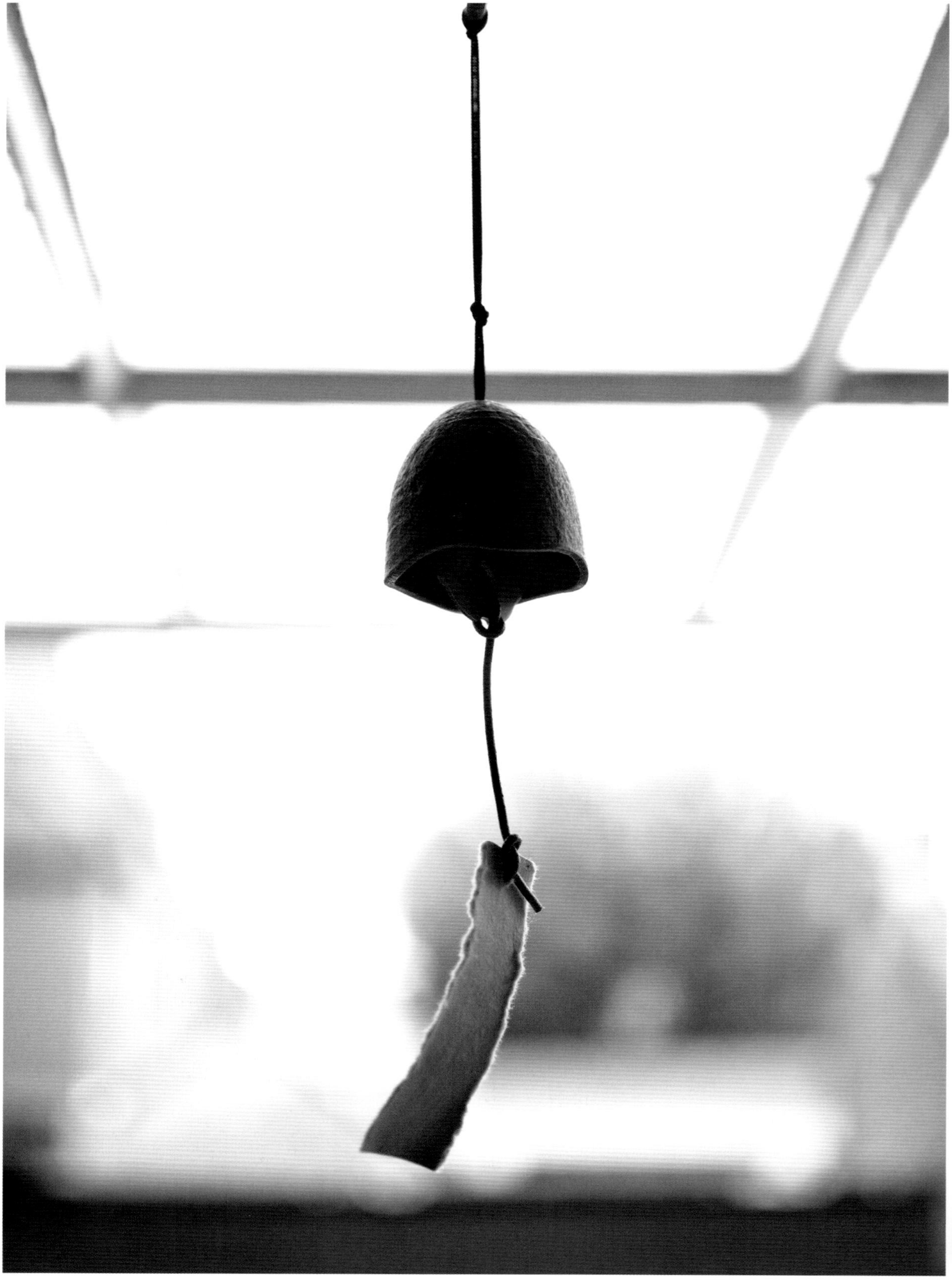

Index

I would like to thank Diana, Anne and Helen for giving me a chance to publish this book. Without them, Sushi Slim would not exist.

To Lucy for her patience and great support. To Lisa for the gorgeous pictures that brought my recipes to life. To Risa for her design and suggestions. To Miki Symons, for her painstaking counting of every calorie in this book!

To Emma for lending me the amazing experience she has collected in her career, and for being there for me for all these years.

To Andrea, Haru, Mai and all Suzu's members for their presence and support.

To my parents Mamoru and Motoko, and my children Eleanor, Leon, Suzu and Verity, for inspiring me and bringing happiness into my life.

And finally, to Simon Matthews, for supporting me all this time and helping me to get this far.

Editorial Director Anne Furniss
Creative Director Helen Lewis
Project Editor Lucy Bannell
Art Direction and Design Mentsen
Photography Lisa Linder
Editorial Consultant Emma Bannister
Dietitian Miki Symons
Food Styling Aya Nishimura
Production Director Vincent Smith
Production Controller Leonie Kellman

First published in 2013 by
Quadrille Publishing Ltd
Alhambra House
27–31 Charing Cross Road
London WC2H 0LS
www.quadrille.co.uk

Text © 2013 Makiko Sano
Photography © 2013 Lisa Linder
Design & layout © 2013 Quadrille Publishing Ltd

British Library Cataloguing-in-Publication Data
A catalogue record for this book is available from the British Library.

ISBN: 978 184949 175 4

Printed in China.